Industrial Archaeological Sites of Britain

Frontispiece Cwmystradllyn slate factory

Industrial Archaeological Sites of Britain

Anthony Burton

Photographs by Clive Coote

Weidenfeld and Nicolson
London

© Anthony Burton 1977

House Editor: Darlene Weber
Designed by Tim Higgins
for George Weidenfeld and Nicolson Ltd
11 St John's Hill, London SW11

ISBN 297 77373 9

Printed in Great Britain
by Butler & Tanner Ltd
Frome and London

Contents

Preface

'Industrial archaeology' is a comparatively new name for a comparatively new subject, and one which can be all things to all men. At one end of the scale is the industrial archaeologist who meticulously studies the remains of old industries, carefully measuring and recording, excavating and testing. His work is indeed very close to that of the traditional archaeologist. At the other end is 'the collector', notching up another mill here, a weavers' cottage there, rather in the manner of small boys collecting train numbers at the end of the platform. In between are those like myself who use the physical remains of buildings and machines much as they use old documents, as aids to an understanding of the past. We are all lumped together under the one title, and the subject with which we are concerned is no more clearly defined. So, before we begin to talk about industrial archaeological sites, it will be as well to define our terms.

So, a definition: industrial archaeology is the process by which we incorporate a study of the physical remains of old industries into the main body of historical research. I have given the word 'industrial' a rather broad meaning. I have, for example, included buildings associated with agriculture, such as grain mills. There are two reasons for this: first the transformation of grain to flour seems to me to be as much an act of manufacture as the transformation of ore into metal; secondly, the technology of windmill and watermill is very important to the whole history of industrial development. I have also included housing, since industrial archaeology is, or should be, at least as concerned with the direct social consequences of industrial change as with industry itself. The inclusion of transport needs no apology. I have, however, imposed some limitations. I shall not be considering anything that began life in this century. Any such limit is necessarily arbitrary, and the end of a century is convenient rather than logical. But it seems to me that limits are needed and mine if no better is at least no worse than any other. Readers will find that the majority of sites fall within the period 1700–1900.

There are literally thousands of sites in Britain which can be classified as industrial archaeological. The industrial revolution began in this country and the remains of that revolution are still to be seen all around us. My main problem has been selection. Take one example – the cotton industry of Lancashire. There are mills, mill villages and even mill towns throughout much of the county. To include them all would have meant a guide ten times the length – and ten times the weight – of this one. So I have tried to select examples which are of particular historical importance, or in some way typify a particular type of development. I have also used some purely subjective criteria. Sometimes, in my travels, I have come across a particular site which has stopped me in my tracks, simply because the different elements seemed to fit so perfectly together, to hold the attention. The building might have had no special significance, but if I found it exciting it went down on the list in the hope that others would share that excitement. Some have found their place simply because I find them beautiful, and there could be many worse reasons than that.

The book is divided between different regions, though the boundaries have more to do with conventional geography than with industrial development. In general, I have tried to follow a logical geographical sequence, but where there are important comparisons to be made I have allowed myself a few small leaps out of the strict sequence. Map references are to the 1:50,000 O.S. map.

I ought to end this preface with a word of warning. The structures described in this book were there when I visited them: I can offer no guarantee they will still be there when you go. In 1974, I published a book, *Remains of a Revolution*, and on the actual day of publication I received a phone call from a Staffordshire paper to say that the bulldozers were moving in on one of my favourite sites that morning. But do not despair. Only recently I went out hunting for a site only to find the demolition squads had been at work, but I kept poking around and finished up at a more exciting site just a mile away. Keep looking then, and I hope you find as much pleasure in these sites as I have.

1 The Beginnings of Industry

Since the majority of the sites listed in this book date from the period 1700–1900, one might be led to suppose that industry mysteriously appeared, a full-grown lusty youth, at some time in the eighteenth century. In fact, there was a very lengthy infancy. The period in the eighteenth century which we now call the industrial revolution can be thought of as the period of puberty, a time marked both by rapid growth and a fundamental change of character. The story of Britain's industrial development cannot be understood without at least taking a brief look at the early infancy.

If you visit the neolithic site known as Grimes Graves at Weeting in Norfolk (TL 817898), you will find the remains of flint mines that date back to the fourth millenium BC. The most striking feature of the area is the scale of activity. This was clearly not just a case of a few men scraping around in the dirt, looking for a suitable flint to fashion into arrow head or knife, but the result of a corporate effort. Here were men getting together, using antler picks and simple tools to produce materials not just for their own immediate use but to serve a wide community. Recent research has shown that flints from Grimes Graves were traded over a very wide area. On site, are shafts that go down as deep as thirty feet, and from the bottom galleries were dug out into the flint. There can be no doubt that at Grimes Graves we are seeing a very early industrial site.

Industrial activity increased with the spread to Britain of metal working somewhere around 2000 BC; first bronze then, more than a thousand years later, iron. Metals were important to the whole development of the ancient world. Iron tools and iron weapons both helped to make life easier for early man, and the metal industry became part of an economy that spread far beyond simple local needs. Technology if not exactly racing forwards was steadily advancing. It received a distinct spur with the Roman occupation. Think of Roman achievement and you think of Roman roads and certainly this is pre-eminent in any discussion of industrial history. Indeed when the Roman occupation finally ended and the country subsided into the Dark Ages, more than a thousand years were to pass before Britain would again see comparable achievements in civil engineering. You can see their work in the straight lines of Watling Street, Akeman Street and the rest. There are also a few places where the road surface still remains. There is a fine example at Blackstone Edge above Little-borough in Lancashire (SD 974172 to SD 987184), but even more inter-esting to the industrial archaeologist is the exposed section at Holyte TQ 461391) near East Grinstead. The surface here is made up of com-pacted slag from the nearby iron works, for this region of Sussex was, and remained throughout medieval times, one of the principal iron-making centres of Britain. When we think of iron-making today, we think of South Wales or Yorkshire, not Sussex and Kent. The centres shifted when man learned, in the eighteenth century, to use coke in-stead of charcoal for smelting. The new industry developed on and around the coalfields, but in earlier times the main requirement was timber, and prodigious quantities of timber at that.

The Romans brought with them to Britain a new device that was to be vital to industrial development – the water wheel. At Chesters on Hadrian's Wall (NY 911700) there is what appears to be a leat dug from the river to divert the water to turn an undershot wheel. Parts of a wheel were found in the River Witham at Lincoln and substantial remnants were discovered on the gold field at Dolaucothi (see p.139). The water wheel was at once seen as a great aid to agriculture, and the miller of grain became an important figure in the rural community. The use of the water wheel to turn millstones has continued over the centuries, but at a very early date the water wheel was put to use turning other things as well. In medieval Britain, the wheel was powering full-ing mills, where newly woven cloth was pounded under great hammers to compact the fibres together; wheels were turning tilt hammers, under which metal was shaped on the anvil; they were powering pumps that worked to drain mines; and when, eventually, the spinning of cot-ton was moved from the home to the factory, it was the water wheel that supplied the power. From grain mill to cotton mill, it is a story of continuous development.

In the past, industrial archaeologists have, not unreasonably, left the excavation of sites of the ancient world to the traditional archaeologist, but no understanding of more recent industrial history would be complete that did not take into account the early years. If there are few early sites listed in this book, it is not because such sites are unimportant but because few have been investigated. I am convinced that industrial archaeology will become more concerned with the earlier period, making more links, more connection between the present and the past.

2 The South-West

Cornwall is as appropriate a place as any to begin a survey of early industrial sites, for if legend is to be believed the Phoenicians came here
to trade for tin. You will find no physical evidence of the activities
of those seafaring gentlemen, but evidence of mining for tin and, more
importantly, for copper, you will find in plenty. The earliest miners
left few traces, for they mostly obtained the tin by streaming, washing
the ore out from alluvial deposits, much in the way the Klondike
miners panned for gold. Mining proper began in the Middle Ages,
when the lodes or veins of ore that outcropped at the surface were
worked. These were mostly near the coast and levels were driven into
the hillside, preferably at an upward slope, so that the tunnels acted
as their own drains. This method gave way eventually to the deep
mines, and with the coming of these mines there also appeared the
great enemy of the miner – water. The answer to that particular problem was to give to Cornwall its most characteristic industrial monument, the engine house. The steam pumping engine brought new life
to Cornish mining, but the story of its development was by no means
untroubled. The first engines, the Newcomen or atmospheric engines
(see p. 22) had prodigious appetites for fuel. This greatly reduced their
usefulness in a county which had no coal of its own. Fuel had to be
brought, at very considerable expense, by sea and then transported,
often over wild, rough country to the mine. The invention of the separate condenser by James Watt brought efficiency to the engine and hope
to the miners. Boulton and Watt engines became common in the
county, but there was bitter resentment over the Midlanders' monopoly. In 1800, when their patent ran out, Cornish engineers began work
in earnest, building ever larger and ever more efficient engines. The
Cornish engine in its distinctive housing was seen not only in Cornwall,
but all over Britain and, eventually, all over the world.

The steam engine arrived just in time for Cornwall. The price of

13

New Mills, Wotton-under-Edge,
beside the mill pond

tin had fallen and miners rioted as they saw their wages reduced to starvation level. Copper was just beginning to replace tin as the main product of mining when the price of copper also plummeted after the discovery that a mountain of copper ore in Anglesey was there for the hacking (see p. 144). Cost was of paramount importance to mine owners, and the solution to the problem of building efficient steam engines marked the beginning of the great period of Cornish prosperity in the nineteenth century. The number and the size of Cornish engines became a measure of Cornish prosperity.

You need travel no more than half a dozen miles from Land's End before you come to one of the old centres of the tin-mining industry. St Just is a village of dour but sturdy granite terraces, around which the mining remains are liberally scattered. There is no better introduction to Cornish mining than a visit to nearby Cape Cornwall. A track leads down from the hamlet of Botallack to the cliffs and the two engine houses of Wheal Edward (sw 360328), which show the characteristics of such buildings. The houses themselves are tall, solid, stone buildings, and the fact that they still stand on such an exposed site is proof of their durability. Beside them are the tall stacks which ensured a good draught to keep the boilers burning brightly. These are stone-built up to the level of the engine house walls for strength, then topped in brick to reduce the load. One wall of the engine house can been seen to be considerably thicker than the other three and to be stained and begrimed with streaks of grease. This is the bob wall. The engines were beam engines. From one end of the beam, the piston rod went down to the cylinder while the other carried the pumping rods, or, in the case of a winding engine used for moving men and materials up and down the shaft, the sweep arm. The great beam, weighing many tons, pivoted on the bob wall. The engine house was more than a mere cover for the engine, it was an integral part of the whole machine.

From Wheal Edward, a walk along the cliffs brings you to the astonishing sight of the two engine houses of Botallack mine (sw 362333). There they perch, half way up the cliff, in an apparently impossible situation. The lower engine house rests on a ledge so small that the stack had to be built inside the house to save space. The engine for this house, built in the 1810s, was a pumping engine with a 30-inch diameter cylinder. All the parts, including the huge granite blocks of the house, had to be lowered from the cliff tops. The upper house was the winding or whim engine house, built to serve the inclined shaft that went down and out under the sea. The romantic location combined with the novelty of an undersea mine to make Botallack a popular Victorian tourist attraction, and Victoria and Albert themselves came to take a look. The site is magnificent, but the point that is made here is that mining was by then so profitable and the steam engine was so essential, that it was worth the while of mining engineers to struggle to overcome the difficulties presented by such a site.

Further on down the coast, is one of the most famous of Cornish mines, Levant (SW 368346). Here, in the little squat engine house, is one of the few surviving beam engines in Cornwall, a 24-inch cylinder engine built by Harveys of Hayle in 1840, but substantially rebuilt in 1862. A whim engine, it is unusual in having the whole engine, beam and flywheel, inside the house; only the drum for the cables that led down the shaft is outside. Walking into the Levant engine house, one gets the feeling that things have only come to a temporary halt, that the engine man will again be seen sitting on the wooden bench inside the door. Outside are some grimmer reminders of Levant's past. Strewn around the area are remnants of the man engine, a series of platforms connected by rods that took men up and down the shaft. In 1919, the engine broke, taking thirty-one miners to their deaths. After the accident, the men used to clamber down the great rift in the cliffs and enter the mine through the adit that can still be seen half way down. Back at the top of the cliffs, there is a confusion of old settling beds, buddles and calciners from the ore dressing plant and the long flues of a later date, when arsenic extraction was an important part of the mine's economy. Today, Levant is again a working site, and evidence of it can be seen in the stain that spreads out at the base of the cliff, turning the sea bright red.

Travelling east along the coast one comes to Hayle, one of the most important industrial towns in Cornwall. It owes its prominence to its geography, set on a land-locked inlet, close to the tin and copper mines and facing out across the channel to South Wales. Hayle had a busy trade, importing coal and exporting ore to the smelters round Swansea. The Cornish were inclined to resent the fact that ore had to be smelted in Wales, and in the 1780s the Copperhouse smelting works were established. However, it was always better economic sense to take the ore to the coal rather than vice versa. Not much remains of the works, but if you look at the canal dock (SW 567380), built as part of the harbour improvement scheme, you will see that it was built up from copper slag. The most important site is at Carnsew, near the centre of the town (SW 558372). It was here that a local smith, John Harvey, established a small ironworks in 1779. In the years after the expiry of the Boulton and Watt patent, Harveys of Hayle gained a reputation for being among the finest engine builders in the country. Their engines can be seen in many different parts of Britain, including the fine engines at Kew (see p. 49). Biggest of them all was the engine sent to Holland to help in draining the Haarlem Mere. The Cruquis engine is preserved and with its vast 144-inch cylinder it stands as a fitting memorial to the work done in this little seaside town.

Inland from Hayle is the important mining area centred around the adjoining towns of Camborne and Redruth. The first stop in Camborne is less of an industrial archaeological halt and more an act of pilgrimage. At Penponds (SW 637389) stands the cottage which was once the home of the pioneer of steam locomotion, Richard Trevithick. In the centre of the town is the Holman Museum, which contains a number of interesting mining exhibits, including a 22-inch, single-acting rotary beam engine from the Rostowrack Clay Works. To the south of the town are the remains of the Basset mines, of which the most extensive are at the South Frances section (SW 680395). The scene is dominated by the engine house that stands by the Marriott shaft. This was a compound engine, that is one with two cylinders: a high pressure cylinder from which the steam passed to the second, low pressure cylinder. This engine, built in 1899, had a 40-inch high-pressure cylinder and an 80-inch low-pressure. It was first fired by four Lancashire boilers, but they proved inadequate and two more were added. The boiler house, with its elaborate arches, has a strangely monastic look. The Basset group as a whole boasts a fine collection of surface buildings, with ore stamps and dressing-floors and, at the main mine, a magnificent bob wall, built of finely dressed granite blocks and dated 1854.

At Pool, between Camborne and Redruth, there are two engines which have been preserved *in situ*. The East Pool whim engine stands beside the A30 (SW 673415). It is a 30-inch rotative beam engine, built by Holmans of Camborne in 1887, which in its working days used to wind down to almost 1500 feet. Across the road, at the Taylor shaft (sw 677417) is East Pool's big brother. This is a 90-inch pumping engine built by Harveys in 1892 and moved to this site in 1924: a massive engine in every sense, with a beam weighing 52 tons. The surrounding area is very liberally bespattered with evidence of mining activity. The little village of St Day on Gwennap Down (sw 730425) was once known as the mining capital of Cornwall, and looking out from its tight clusters of terraced cottages, one sees everywhere the spoil heaps and engine houses that tell of a once thriving industry. The most interesting, and historically the most important site is Wheal Busy (sw 741448). There has been a succession of no fewer than ten engines on this site, starting with a Newcomen engine installed in 1725. At that date, the mine was under the control of John Carter, 'the father of Cornish copper mining', who was among the first to turn from the traditional tin working to the more complex problem of copper extraction. The present engine house was built in 1856 to hold an 85-inch engine, and is one of the few houses still to have its single-storey boiler house attached.

This area was served by the Redruth and Chacewater Railway, built in 1824. It was a typical mineral railway of the period, designed to carry horse-drawn trucks. The metal rails were carried on stone sleeper blocks. Much of the old line can be traced through the mining region, but it can be seen at its best near Twelveheads (sw 7642), where the line went down into a deep cutting.

One could go on almost indefinitely, it seems, listing Cornish mine sites, so we shall concentrate on a few more which deserve a special mention. The valley that leads away from the sea at Porthtowan was once rich in copper ore, and today is heavily scarred from generations of workings. It is especially interesting because of the wildness of the setting, a reminder of the great problems posed to the engineers. The engine houses remain as monuments to the efforts made to surmount the difficulties. Here is United Hills with two engine houses: the lower (sw 698473) comparatively small and ruinous and reputed to have held the last engine to be built with a wooden instead of an iron beam; the upper grand and aloof, high above the valley (sw 702472). Deeper into the valley is one of the few houses that has made any concession to aesthetics, for the top of the stack has been crenellated.

Back at the coast is another once-famous mining centre, St Agnes.

The South-West

For those who like a little romanticism with their industry, here is an area to rival Cape Cornwall, with Wheal Coates (SW 700501) high up on the cliffs winning the prize for the most romantic setting. The town itself is well worth exploring. During the nineteenth century almost 200,000 tons of copper ore were produced from mines within the parish boundary. The Miners and Mechanics Institute, a plain, unprepossessing building, has a large stock of photographs showing the district in its working days. One still seems to find engine houses everywhere, even, rather surprisingly, in someone's back garden. Wheal Kitty (SW 726509) is particularly interesting, for besides having the inevitable engine house, it still has the old count house where miners used to come and bid for the work at the mines. The Cornish miner was not, in the early days, a salaried employee. He took out a contract to work a particular section, and was paid either by measurement of the area cleared or in terms of the value of the ore removed. The rate for the job was decided at public auction, held outside the count house and a man's earnings depended on his skill as a worker and on his skill in assessing the potential of a particular section. It made for independence but could also lead to destitution. If he fixed too low a price, he could find himself labouring for months with no reward at the end.

Over on the other side of the peninsula, evidence of another industrial activity is equally inescapable. Here are the 'Cornish Alps', the huge white hills of spoil that dominate the skyline, the debris of the china-clay industry. This is an industry that first came into prominence in the late eighteenth century, when William Cookworthy took out a patent for the use of china clay in the manufacture of porcelain. When his monopoly was broken, the Staffordshire potters, led by Josiah Wedgwood, invaded Cornwall in force and the china clay industry began to boom. Its continued success has meant, in many cases, that old remains have simply disappeared before the advance of the new technology. The water-powered mills where china stone was ground have all gone, though at St Stephen-in-Brannel (SW 949552) are the remains of a series of five mills, all fed from the same water source, the water falling from mill to mill. The finest of the remaining historical sites is certainly Wheal Martyn (SX 005555). Here you can still see a 'Cornish lift', a beam pump which was operated by an overshot water wheel. The clay was pumped up in the form of a slurry, then passed down through a series of settling tanks to the drying kilns. On this one small site, all the different processes of the industry can be traced.

The main users of china clay were the Staffordshire potters, so a new port, Charlestown, was built for the local landowner Charles Rashleigh (SX 040515). The harbour was designed by John Smeaton and completed in 1798. It is in two parts: an outer harbour enclosed by two quays and an inner harbour protected by lock gates. The port is still in use and china clay is still loaded through gravity chutes. Nearby (SX 038519) is Rashleigh's foundry, where many of the engines used in the surrounding clay pits were manufactured. It remains in use, but does retain some relics of its earlier days including a fine, pitch-back water wheel, 30-feet in diameter, that once powered the tilt hammers in the works.

The china clay industry is concentrated in this one small region, and one has only to move away a short distance before finding oneself back among the tin and copper mines. The Cheesewring on Bodmin Moor offers a curiosity. South Phoenix engine house (SX 260717) was built in 1853 to take a 50-inch engine from Nicholls Williams of Tavistock. When the engine stopped work, the house was converted first to a store then to a home, and you can still see odd details, such as the little domestic chimney pots. Nearby is the much grander engine house of Phoenix United (SX 262725), built for a tin mine in this predominantly copper-mining area. Here one of Cornwall's last big pumping engines was installed in 1908 in a vain attempt to restore the old days of prosperity. The house is an exceptionally fine three-storey building of locally quarried stone which housed an 80-inch engine by Holmans of Camborne. It was started by the Prince of Wales, but royal patronage failed to bring royal fortunes. There are extensive remains of boiler house, dressing-floors and stamps.

Phoenix United lay on the route of the Liskeard–Caradon railway, built soon after copper was found in South Caradon in 1837. In 1844 it was joined to the Looe Canal, so that ore could be sent on to the port. The line follows a contour round Caradon Hill in a great sweeping curve, and can be clearly traced on its way through the mines of the south side of the hill (SX 273698). This is one of the oldest copper-mining areas in the region and well worth exploring. There are three engine houses and the last man engine to be used in Cornwall was installed here. Further west, at Kelly Bray (SX 356711) is a very attractive site, with a small ivy-covered engine house and a larger neighbour which contained a 60-inch engine built at Tavistock in Devon. But as the engine was built after the Tavistock company was taken over, the name on the tie beams let into the wall is that of the Bedford Foundary. Finally, in this area, the stack at the top of Kit Hill (SX 375713) was built both to do a job of work for the mine and to stand as a monument to the Cornish miners.

Quite the most spectacular way to make the crossing from Cornwall into Devon is via Brunel's Royal Albert railway bridge at Saltash (SX 4260). The height and great width were insisted upon by the Admiralty, who wanted the Tamar kept clear for navigation. It was first considered in the 1840s, but work was delayed and the bridge was not finally opened until 1859, by which time Brunel was so ill that he had to be taken across on an invalid couch set on a flat truck. A few weeks later he was dead and the Saltash bridge stands as his last great work. It is a fitting memorial on the grand scale: each of the two main spans is 465-feet long and weighs over 1,500 tons. The construction method devised by Brunel was a mixture between the suspension and the bowstring systems. The main load is carried by huge curved iron tubes from which the rail deck is suspended by chains.

Further down the Tamar is the old port of Morwellham, which has recently been made into an industrial museum. The water has long since retreated from the quays, leaving bollards and wharves quite literally high and dry. But there is enough evidence in the warehouses, ore-crushing plant and lime kilns to give an indication of just how busy the port once was. The ore came from the mines near Tavistock. In 1796, John Taylor opened up Wheal Friendship (SX 508794) and the workings were sufficiently rich to justify the construction of a whole new transport system. The result was the Tavistock Canal, the main feature of which was a mile-long narrow tunnel. During construction, tests were made for ore deposits along the route with the result that the Crebor group of mines was established. From the southern end of the tunnel, the canal passes round the shoulder of the hill to end at an inclined plane that took the ore down to the harbour. There are substantial remains of the incline, including a large number of stone sleeper blocks. In later years, the main traffic in the harbour came from the Devon Great Consul mines: when they closed the harbour closed too.

Copper mining continues on into Devon and Dartmoor, but there it is soon rivalled in importance by another great industry of the West Country, stone quarrying. The best known of all the quarries is that at Haytor (sx 755775), from which stone was taken for the old London Bridge. It is also notable for having the country's most unusual railway – the Haytor Granite Tramway. Odd it may be, but it was a practical enough system. In 1820, when the quarries were opened, the owners were faced with the familiar problem of transport through difficult country. A railway was an obvious answer, but metal rails were expensive and difficult to come by so they hit upon the ingenious idea of constructing their railway entirely from granite blocks. That the system was successful and durable can easily be gauged from the very substantial sections that still remain, leading away from the quarries. Of course, the use of local granite to ease the problems of transport was no new thing on Dartmoor. In the early days, when the pack animal did all the carrying for the region, simple bridges were constructed by supporting slabs of stone on piers made up of piled stones. These are known as clapper bridges, and probably the best example can be seen at Portbridge (sx 648789), where the bridge has stood for some seven hundred years.

On the northern edge of Dartmoor stands the village of Sticklepath, which at first sight appears much like any other Devon village. Yet, in its day, this was a busy industrial centre where heavy woollen serge was manufactured. Of the many mills that were once powered by the River Taw only Cleave Mill (sx 640940) still stands. But the most interesting site in the village relates to agriculture rather than woollen cloth. The Finch Foundry was begun in one of the old serge mills in 1814 and here, for a century and a half, agricultural tools were manufactured for the surrounding district. Why it was called 'Foundry' is a mystery, for all the work was done by forging not casting.

Little has changed at Finch's over the years. Power is still supplied by a series of overshot water wheels, turned by water from the Taw which is carried to the site on a wooden launder. Edge tools can still be made here in just the way they were made in 1814. The process starts at the lower end of the works, where the third wheel turns the fan that provides the draught for the hearths in the adjoining hammer room. Here the metal is heated, then shaped under trip hammers and drop hammers, powered by the second wheel. The tilt hammers are worked by means of a turning wheel with a projection that hits the end of the hammer, lifts it and then as the wheel turns, the hammer is released to fall back on the anvil. At one time this room was connected to a saw mill, where handles were made, but this has been demolished. The third wheel turns the grindstone on which the tools were sharpened. It looks an alarming process, for the grinder lies full length holding the tool down to the stone below him. Parts of this plant may look as if they were designed by Mr Heath Robinson, but in its active days five men could turn out 400 swan-neck hoes in a single day.

Dartmouth was the home of one of the great pioneers of the industrial revolution, Thomas Newcomen, the inventor of the atmospheric engine. In the Newcomen engine, steam was condensed in a cylinder by spraying it with cold water, creating a partial vacuum. Air pressure then forced down the piston which was attached to an overhead beam. Pumping rods, suspended from the other end of the beam were thus raised. When equilibrium was reached in the cylinder, the weight of the rods pulled the beam back down the other way to complete the cycle. So a regular rocking motion was achieved. It was an uneconomical device as heat was wasted through the cylinder being alternately heated and cooled, but a robust one. A Newcomen engine has been re-erected, in a specially constructed engine house, in the middle of the town as a monument to the engineer (sx 878514). Originally it stood at Hawkesbury Junction, where the Oxford and Coventry Canals meet, and the original engine house still stands though the boiler house was recently demolished. While on the subject of canals, it is worth mentioning the Exeter Canal, where the now familiar 'pound lock' was first introduced into Britain by John Trew at the remarkably early date of 1564. But the canal we see today dates from a reconstruction and widening in 1701.

Dorset can boast stone quarries even more famous than those of Devon – the Portland Quarries, source of the white Portland stone. The main quarries are out near the end of the Bill (sy 6972), but all along the eastern side, the cliff top is strewn with the quarried stone, piled up like giant building blocks. The moving of the huge blocks represented an immense labour, which was much eased with the building of the Merchants' Railway in 1825. It ran around the cliffs, ending in an inclined plane that dropped down to the harbour and which is still a prominent landmark today.

Somerset is a county which, today, is thought of as primarily rural but which, in the past, was the scene of much industrial activity. In the Mendips, that activity goes back at least as far as the Roman occupation, when lead ore was extracted from the ground and smelted to extract the metal. The area around Charterhouse shows the evidence of extensive workings in the much disturbed ground (ST 5055). The area was all but exhausted by the end of the seventeenth century, and there was little activity until Cornish engineers arrived with new smelting techniques and began resmelting the old slag heaps. Most of the visible remains of the industry are connected with this period. The Priddy lead works (ST 545505) give the clearest idea of the system involved. A track leads past a small stone-built office that marks the entrance to the site towards a landscape of spoil heaps, dotted with the foundations of old buildings. The most interesting surviving features are the flues that lead out from the ruined smelters. Lead is very volatile and these exceptionally long flues were needed to ensure condensation. The dark, dripping tunnels can still be explored – but only by those properly equipped for the job.

The city that dominates this region is Bristol and, for the industrial archaeologist, the man who dominates that city is Isambard Kingdom Brunel. At the age of twenty-four, he entered into competition with such notable engineers as Thomas Telford for the design of a bridge across the Avon Gorge. He won – and anyone seeing the other designs, especially Telford's Gothic monster, must be grateful that he did. Clifton suspension bridge (ST 563730) is majestic, elegant and justly famous. The piers were completed in 1836, but then cash ran out and the bridge was not finally opened until 1864 by which time Brunel was dead. It retained its connections with the engineer right to the end, however, for the chains came from Brunel's footbridge over the Thames at Charing Cross.

The main achievement that one associates with Brunel is, of course, the building of the Great Western Railway. Temple Meads Station (ST 598725) has been much altered over the years, but the old train shed remains, even though it now suffers the indignity of serving as

Above left
ss *Great Britain*

Left
Carved inscription at
Saltford Mill, marking
the start of work on
the Avon and Gloucester
Railway branch at
Keynsham

Above The two engine houses
on the cliffs at Botallack

Above
Gloucester Docks

Above left
The Handle House,
where teazles were
stored, Studley Mill,
Trowbridge

Left
The Cotswold woollen
mill – Egypt Mill,
Nailsworth

Right
The remains of
the water wheel at
Rode Mill

a car park. The wooden roof has a 72-foot span, wider even than West-minster Hall, and one can still imagine the scene when the old broad gauge still ran beneath its arch. Finest of all the monuments to Brunel that the city can boast is one that began life here, looks like ending its days here, but had a very chequered history in between. Work on the ss *Great Britain* began when the keel was laid in July 1839, and from the first it was an exciting project, for the ship was to be built of iron rather than the conventional wood. But it was only after work began that Brunel took the momentous decision to change from the original plan of building a paddle steamer to one which would be driven by a screw propeller. One can hardly overestimate the importance of the decision, and the *Great Britain* has its place in the history books as the world's first screw-propelled ship. It served successfuly as liner, cargo vessel and troopship before it was abandoned in the Falkland Islands in 1886. Now it has been brought back to the dry dock where it started life (ST 575722). Restoration work has been slow but reas-suringly steady. The emphasis, at first, was on restoring the hull, but now other parts have been returned to something very close to their former glory. The bows, with figurehead, trailboard and bowsprit are today the most striking features and a good deal of work has been done on the transom and stern face. The forecastle has been redecked, the funnel installed, and, most importantly, a replica propeller fitted. By the end of 1977 it is expected that the main mast will be in place, the poop redecked and fitted out and gunwales added. One day, fates and finances willing, ss *Great Britain* will be fully restored, and what a day for celebration that will be.

Bristol was once a centre for the copper and brass industries, and there are many remains of this once thriving trade spread out down the banks of the Avon. One of the few sites where a whole complex of buildings remains intact is the Swineford Copper Works (ST 691690), which date from the 1840s. There are two main ranges of buildings with two undershot water wheels and a very fine mill house attached to the site. Nearby are two particularly interesting brass works. Kelston Works (ST 693680) still has two annealing ovens where the copper and zinc were heated. They are tall, tapered structures of Bath stone with rubble walls and dressed stone at the quoins. Origin-ally, there were six water wheels on the site, powering the various cut-ting- and slitting-machines. All but one of the watercourses have been covered over as the site was subject to flooding and the present owners have raised the floor level. There are no other surface remains of great interest, though a good deal of the wharf area has been cleared. This is not the case at Saltford Mill (ST 688670). Here, the single annealing oven still has its workshop around it, a stone built building with timber roof supports and cast-iron windows. The furnace is ruinous but still has much of its old hearth. An adjoining building has an iron water wheel and sections of drive shafting. There is a good deal to see here, including large slag blocks and an inscription on a wall which reads 'Begun Diggin The Rail Road Juncn 1836', which presumably refers to the extension of the Avon and Gloucestershire Railway to a wharf near Keynsham.

Moving up river, transport continues to provide the dominant interest. At Bath, the Avon is crossed by a suspension bridge (ST 741650) which if not as dramatic as that at Clifton is nevertheless of considerable interest. The suspension rods are inclined towards the piers, a method of construction which Dredge, the bridge's designer, patented. Bath also marks the start of the Kennet and Avon Canal, built to link the Thames to the Severn. The chief engineer was John Rennie, who supplied the canal with some splendid architecture but, sadly, seldom enough water. One method of remedying that defect can be seen at Claverton (ST 792643) where an old water mill was converted into a pumping station. Water from the Avon turns a breast-shot wheel which, in turn, powers the beam pumps. The wheel is a composite with wooden paddles on a 19-foot iron frame, and is regulated by a 5-ton flywheel. So the power of water is used to lift water 53-feet up the hillside and into the canal. From one elegant solution to a problem to another: the Dundas Aqueduct (ST 784626) which carries the canal across the Avon. It is a good example of Rennie's penchant for the classical style. The river is spanned by a single arch, balanced by smaller arches on either side. The decoration consists of Doric columns, a deep cornice and a balustraded parapet, all built of the same lovely Bath stone. The basin at the southern end of the aqueduct marks the point where the Somerset Coal Canal came in. There is a small crane and warehouse and higher up the hill is a tollhouse that once stood beside the locks. Conveniently close at hand for comparison purposes is a viaduct, reputedly by Telford, which carries the Limpley Stoke road over Milford Brook (ST 782621). It is an elegant enough structure, but has none of the panache of the Dundas. From canal and road, one can go on and complete the transport trilogy with one of the most impressive of railway engineering feats, the 3,272-yard-long Box Hill tunnel. The end nearest to Bath (ST 830689) has been given an appropriately fine classical entrance.

As Somerset meets Wiltshire, one arrives at an area which was once among the most heavily industrialized of the whole country, the area of woollen cloth manufacture. In the days before cotton came to rule the textile kingdom, woollen cloth was a major industrial product, serving a steady home demand and a thriving export trade. The West of England, with its ample pasture land for sheep and clear streams to turn the mills was an ideal centre. From Somerset and Wiltshire up into Gloucestershire the remains are everywhere to be seen and they present us with some of the loveliest as well as some of the most interesting industrial relics.

A good place to begin is Dilton Marsh (ST 8550) to the south of Trowbridge. This is a squatters' village. Weavers came here, attracted by a booming trade, and built their straggles of cottages on the common land along the main road. Some were single cottages, others formed groups and terraces – but all had some space set aside for the hand looms that earned them their living, either in the house itself or in outhouses. The cloth from the weavers was sent to the fulling mills that lined the rivers of the district, where it was scoured and cleaned and pounded under the water-powered hammers, the fulling stocks, until it had shrunk and matted. There are many of these early mills to be seen, though many have served a multiplicity of uses over the years. Shawford Mill (ST 793533) is a good and very attractive example. Mills have stood on this site for centuries, though the present stone mill dates from the early 1800s. It is a two-storey building with nine bays of mullioned windows and still possesses a small water wheel, now used for generating electricity. It seems probable that the building originally also served as a gig mill, that is one in which machinery was used to raise the nap of the cloth and then trim it smooth. Further up the same river is Rode Mill (ST 802543), a typical small mill, plain and functional. Parts of the water wheel can still be seen and, like many mills in the area, when the cloth trade declined it was adapted for use as a grain mill. Tellisford offers one not only the remains of a woollen mill (ST 806557) but also a picture of the sort of transport system that

30

served the industry. Here the old pack-horse route crosses the river by means of a narrow stone bridge before turning onto a cobbled route up the steep hillside.

The two main urban centres for this southern part of the cloth industry were Bradford-on-Avon and Trowbridge. The town centre of Bradford now has few reminders of its industrial past, though the fine houses built by the clothiers in the area and known as the Torys provide eloquent testimony that that past was a wealthy one. The surviving mills are impressive. Kingston and Greenland Mills (ST 828608) are on the river to the east of the town. Trowbridge, by contrast, still has working woollen mills in the centre of the town and has a number of historically interesting sites. Perhaps the most interesting of these are the humblest, the weavers' homes. Where the squatters of Dilton Marsh had room to spread, the town weavers, faced with high land costs, could only build upwards. So we find second-floor workshops, easily recognized by the long 'weavers' windows', designed to provide maximum light for the loom (ST 857582). The cramped terraces are in marked contrast to the many grand houses built by the more opulent merchants. Among the many mills in the town, the most interesting is Studley (ST 855575). The original clothier's house stands immediately inside the main gate, a handsome dignified building showing all the grace of the eighteenth century. Behind it is an incoherent jumble of workshops where the spinners and weavers plied their craft. Then mechanization came in, in the shape of the tall, nineteenth-century mill building. Spinning, weaving and cloth-dressing were taken from the home to the factory. An important part of the manufacturing process involved raising the nap of the cloth. This was done using teazles, at first wielded by hand then, mounted on a roller, in the gig mill. At Studley, the teazles were stored in the 'handle house' which straddles the river; built of brick it has perforated walls to help the drying process.

The West of England was an area where innovations were often strongly resisted by the domestic workers. One solution was to move the business to a safer area. Francis Hill left Bradford-on-Avon in 1790 and established a mill for spinning wool at Malmesbury (ST 936869). Avon Mill is an almost perfect example of an eighteenth-century spinning mill. It is an L-shaped stone building, five storeys high with eight bays in each wing. The shape is tall and narrow to take the rows of spinning-machines, each belt driven from the drive shafts that ran down the middle of each wing. The mill was water-powered and the sluice gates controlling the water can still be seen.

North of Malmesbury, on the edge of the Cotswolds, is the town of Stroud, centre of the Gloucestershire woollen trade. In and around the town, strung out along every river and tributary, the mills stood. Even today there are quite literally hundreds of mills remaining, some altogether ruinous, others virtually intact. Here we can do no more than look at a few outstanding examples – and outstanding is what they certainly are. Two examples can be seen at Wotton-under-Edge. Town Mill (ST 756935) is, as the name suggests, in the centre of the town and is one of the very few in the area to be built specifically as a steam-powered mill. The visitor to New Mills (ST 737929) can be in no doubt that the mill was originally water-powered, for the first thing he sees is the big mill pond, fed by a half mile leat. This is one of the rare brick-built mills in a predominantly stone area, but it is an imposing building, four storeys high with attic, and embellished by a splendid gabled staircase tower with a handsome clock. The circular building that now holds the reception office was once the wool stove, where wool was dried, and a small stone count house still stands by the main building.

The greatest concentration of mills is to be found in the river valleys centred on Stroud. Longford Mill (ST 867992) provides a very good example of the way in which a mill complex could change and develop over the years. The oldest part, characterized by a little ogee arched window carries two dates, 1705 and 1866. There is a four-storey mill building dating from the eighteenth century, a two-storey building with engine house that marks the coming of steam in the nineteenth century and new weaving sheds that were added early in this century. Nearby Dunkirk Mill (ST 845005) also shows successive expansions, but here the changes are less immediately obvious. Instead of adding new buildings, existing buildings were extended, yet each extension kept to the same line and used similar materials, so that an overall unity was preserved. Once there were four water wheels, but now only the water courses and sluices remain. There is an attractive mill house, and by the entrance is a small warehouse where a former occupant, Peter Playne, inscribed his initials and the date 1829 on a keystone.

Between these two grand mills stands the much smaller Egypt Mill

(ST 848999), named after a seventeenth-century owner, Pharoah Webb. It is a delightful building, consisting of two connected stone ranges, each two storeys high and roofed in Cotswold stone slate. Once a fulling mill, it has been converted into a grain mill, but much of the old machinery, including the two internal water wheels, has survived. That even a small mill such as this could generate a good deal of wealth can be seen from the gabled clothier's house next door.

Continuing north, one reaches Frogmarsh Mill (ST 841018) which again offers a jumble of styles and periods, so patched and altered that it appears to offer little of interest. But there are curiosities, such as the cog wheel that has found a new use as a tie-beam end, and the weavers' windows at the northern end of the mill, suggesting that hand looms were once worked here. The main feature of interest, however, stands across the road – the last wool stove in the area to survive virtually intact. It is circular with pointed arches and a conical roof.

Turning west out of Stroud one reaches Ebley Mill (SO 825045), which is something of a curiosity in having a tower attached to the main block which seems to have been borrowed from a French *château*. This part of the works is the New Mill, built in 1818, while the other blocks are of slightly earlier date. In the 1830s, the works were bought by the Marling family who also acquired Stanley Mill (SO 812043). If Ebley Mill is an architectural oddity, then Stanley is an architectural marvel, arguably the country's most elegant industrial building. It was brick built in 1813 as a fireproof mill, with brick floors and an iron frame. The builders' great achievement was in uniting the practical virtues of the iron frame with the decorative possibilities of cast iron. Instead of plain iron supports, they had pillars cast with elaborate iron arches springing from them. At the lower levels the pillars are massive, but at the higher levels the slender colonnades would not disgrace the stateliest of stately homes. The decorative possibilities of the iron work were further explored in details such as windows – Venetian windows with little columns in the recesses, intricate fan lights, and even a rose window. But however intricate the decoration becomes it is always tied to some functional need in the building. Behind the mill is the Stroudwater Canal, along which the cast iron parts were shipped from the Earl of Dudley's works.

Turning back east one comes to St Mary's Mill, Minchinhampton (SO 885023), which is yet another site where a long history of cloth making can be traced: the first record of a fulling mill dates back to 1548. Today, the oldest remains are from the early nineteenth century, but the old water mill is a fine example of Cotswold vernacular building and there is an equally fine house that was once the home of the mill owner. This mill stands beside the Thames and Severn Canal, and at nearby Chalford is one of the distinctive circular canal cottages (SO 893023). Its similarity to the wool stoves that were once a commonplace in the area can scarcely be a coincidence.

The Thames and Severn connected with the Stroudwater Canal and through that with the Gloucester and Sharpness Ship Canal, built to bypass the dangerous shoals and sandbanks of the Severn. Sharpness is the southern terminal. The canal was first opened in 1827, but the old lock (SO 670030) proved inadequate for a growing trade and larger boats, so in 1871 a new dock was begun and a new inland port complex was created. The new ship lock (SO 668022) was far larger than the old, and new port facilities were built to cope with larger cargoes. The warehouses still stand, simple but impressive, even if today they are somewhat dwarfed by the modern grain silo. The other terminal, Gloucester, is even more impressive, for in Gloucester docks (SO 826185) we have a nineteenth-century port installation which has scarcely changed since it was built. The tall warehouses range all the way round the docks, mostly plain, functional buildings, though there is a distinctive touch to the Pillar Warehouse, which has its upper storeys projecting out over the towpath and wharf on massive pillars.

Turning back again towards the south-west, we come to the most important of the sites connected with the Great Western Railway – Swindon. Sharpness was a canal town, brought into being by the canal – the railway did the same for New Swindon. It was here that Brunel built his engine works and repair sheds, and around them the new town was planned. Unlike many of its contemporaries, Swindon was designed with a sense of style. Recent renovation has brought out the quality of the stone terraces, overlooked by the handsome church of St Mark's in the fashionable Gothic revival style and the secular towers of the Institute, now the railway museum. The new town stands much as it was a century ago, even if it is no longer surrounded by fields. The station, however, designed by Matthew Digby Wyatt, has been modernized and its appearance drastically altered – and not, I would suggest, for the better.

Further south, we rejoin the older transport route of the Kennet and Avon Canal. At Devizes, the canal climbs the hillside by the twenty-nine broad locks of the Caen Hill flight (ST 9862). This is not the largest flight in the country, but even in its present derelict condition it is the most dramatic. Each broad lock has its own individual reservoir of water, in the form of a side pond terraced into the hill, and almost the entire flight can be seen in a single view. Moving east along the canal, we reach Crofton pumping station (SU 264625) and we end this section as we began it, with the steam engine. Here two engines were installed to pump water from a nearby lake up into the summit level of the canal. One of the engines is Cornish, but the second is one of the original Boulton and Watt engines, installed in 1812. This is a remarkably interesting engine, for not only is it still in working order, but it can still perform the work it was installed to do. The engines are in the care of the Crofton Engine Society and both are regularly steamed, giving the spectator a demonstration of the great power of even quite small engines. The 6-ton beams begin to nod, the pump rods move and water gushes. When both these engines were working flat out, they could shift six and a half million gallons in twenty-four hours, during which time the boilers would use up a ton and a quarter of coal. The working engines also give an opportunity to admire the skill and ingenuity of the engineers: there is Watt's parallel linkage, which enables the piston rod to keep a nearly vertical line even though the beam end to which it is attached describes the arc of a circle, and there is the system of levers that act automatically to open and close valves in the correct sequence. Or one can simply marvel at the world's oldest steam engine that is still capable of carrying on its original task. How many of today's machines will be capable of work a century and a half from now?

3 The South and the East

Of all the regions of Britain, this large area is the one least associated with industrial development. On the other hand, it is an area with strong connections with agriculture and is particularly well stocked with grain mills of many different types. Most of the examples listed over the next few pages will be windmills, mainly because the water wheel was applied to so many different processes that it is adequately dealt with in other sections. One exception, however, is the tide mill. The internal machinery of the tide mill is no different from that of the conventional water mill, since the only difference between the two lies in the method of ensuring a regular water supply to turn the wheel. The tidal water, rising up a creek or estuary, fills the mill pond and can then be released in the normal manner through sluices. The system can be seen very clearly at Beaulieu (SU 388023), a small but very attractive two-storey brick mill with dormer windows and weather boarding at the rear. On the road frontage there is a central loading bay and hoist. The undershot wheel drove two pairs of stones, and though the machinery is now in very poor condition, there are plans for restoration.

North of Beaulieu, at Whitchurch, there is a last reminder of the West of England cloth trade. The mill (SU 462479) has since changed from wool-spinning to silk, but the change has in no way affected the appearance of the mill. It is a three-storey building, very stylish and very obviously Georgian with its central pediment and ornate cupola. The River Test divides to flow on either side of the mill, and the waters of the Test turn the breast-shot wheel, which still has its drive mechanism intact. Altogether this is a most attractive site.

Moving south-east again, the impression given to the traveller is one of passing through a predominantly rural landscape, which makes it all the more surprising when one comes across an industrial site which, in terms of the history of technology, is of quite outstanding

Union Mill, lording it over Cranbrook

importance. This area, once covered in forest, was, in the days when charcoal was exclusively used for smelting iron ore, the centre of British iron making. It was after the industry had already begun to decline that Henry Cort took over a small ironworks near Fareham (SU 550070) in 1775. Here he developed a technique for turning the brittle cast iron, obtained from the blast furnace, into the more malleable wrought iron, using coal as the fuel. The problem lies in removing the carbon impurities, and this was achieved by melting the cast iron in a reverberatory furnace – that is, a furnace in which the heat is not applied directly, but by hot gases passed over the metal. The molten metal is stirred, 'puddled', with iron bars, which pass through holes in the brickwork of the furnace. The iron forms into clods, which can be removed and rolled into bars. Charcoal no longer had any part to play in the iron industry, and the forges could join the furnaces on the coal fields. Little now remains of Cort's works, but part of a reverberatory furnace can be seen with the holes for the puddlers' rods.

Cort's work speeded up the decline of the iron industry that once thrived in the Sussex Weald until it finally disappeared – but not without trace. Take any of the 1:50,000 O.S. maps of the region, sheet no. 198 for example, and you will find patches of water marked with such names as Hammer Pond, Furnace Pond and New Pond. The ponds are generally seen to be in the shape of a long triangle, a clear indication that they were man-made from dammed up streams. It was from such ponds that water once fell onto the water wheels that worked the bellows for furnace and forge or lifted the big tilt hammers under which the metal was worked. Visit any of these ponds and you will find that the sheer size of them gives an indication of the size of the works. You can also see in the thick woods that surround many of the ponds, one of the principal raw materials of the iron-making process, the timber from which the charcoal was made. So heavy was the use of timber that Daniel Defoe recorded in the early eighteenth century that people began 'to complain of the consuming of it for those furnaces, and leaving the next age to want timber for building their navies'. In many cases, the ponds are all that remain of the once busy industry, but in some places more substantial remains can be found. Look, for example, at the furnace pond to the north of Cowfold (TQ 228247). The track from the road leads down to a substantial bridge that crosses the stream at the point where water now pours through the ruined sluices. Close by is a large masonry wall and what appears to be a section of a hearth, judging by the scorch marks. In many ways it is a typical site, overgrown and ruinous, but one which, like many another, would repay careful examination and excavation. There is still a good deal of field work to be done on the Sussex iron industry.

From iron making we return to the grinding of corn, for this part of southern England is particularly well endowed with windmills. Shipley Mill (TQ 143218) is probably the finest smock mill in the country. This type of mill has a moveable top section – the cap – which carries the sails. The cap also carries a small fan tail which spins busily in the wind and which is in turn attached to a winding mechanism that turns the cap to keep the sails correctly aligned into the wind. She – windmills share the feminine gender with boats – was built in 1879 by the appropriately named millwrights, Grist and Steel of Horsham. Inside the mill, the machinery is intact and shows the principal features which are basically the same for most large mills. The horizontal rotation of the main wind shaft is converted to rotation of the main vertical shaft by means of a gear that engages with a large horizontal wheel, the wallower, set at the top of the shaft. Lower down the shaft is the great spur wheel which supplies power to three pairs of stones through smaller gears, the stone nuts. Other devices such as the sack hoist can be driven by similar use of gears. Speed can be regulated by a simple governor. At one time, this mill was driven by a steam-engine that was housed in the small shed at the side of the mill. One final point, which is of literary rather than industrial interest – the mill was once owned by Hilaire Belloc.

Nutley Mill (TQ 451291) presents a decided contrast with Shipley. This is a post mill, the oldest and simplest form of European windmill. Here the whole mill pivots on a central post and is heaved bodily round, by means of a long, projecting tail pole, to face into the wind. Obviously such mills had to be considerably smaller than the smock mills, and Nutley is one of the smallest in the country, a plain weather-boarded building which was probably built around 1800. The date 1817 can be seen carved on a beam inside. The mill has recently been restored to working order, and occasionally the sails again turn in the wind.

Nutley showed the post mill at its plainest. Argos Hill Mill, Maysfield (TQ 571283) is altogether more elaborate. Like the smock mill, it no longer depends on brute force to move it into position. The end

Above
Three Mills Lane at Bow:
the Tide Mill is on
the left, the distillery
on the right

Above left
Hook Norton brewery

Left
The woodworking shop
at Combe Mill awaiting
restoration

Right
The transept of the great
roof at Paddington

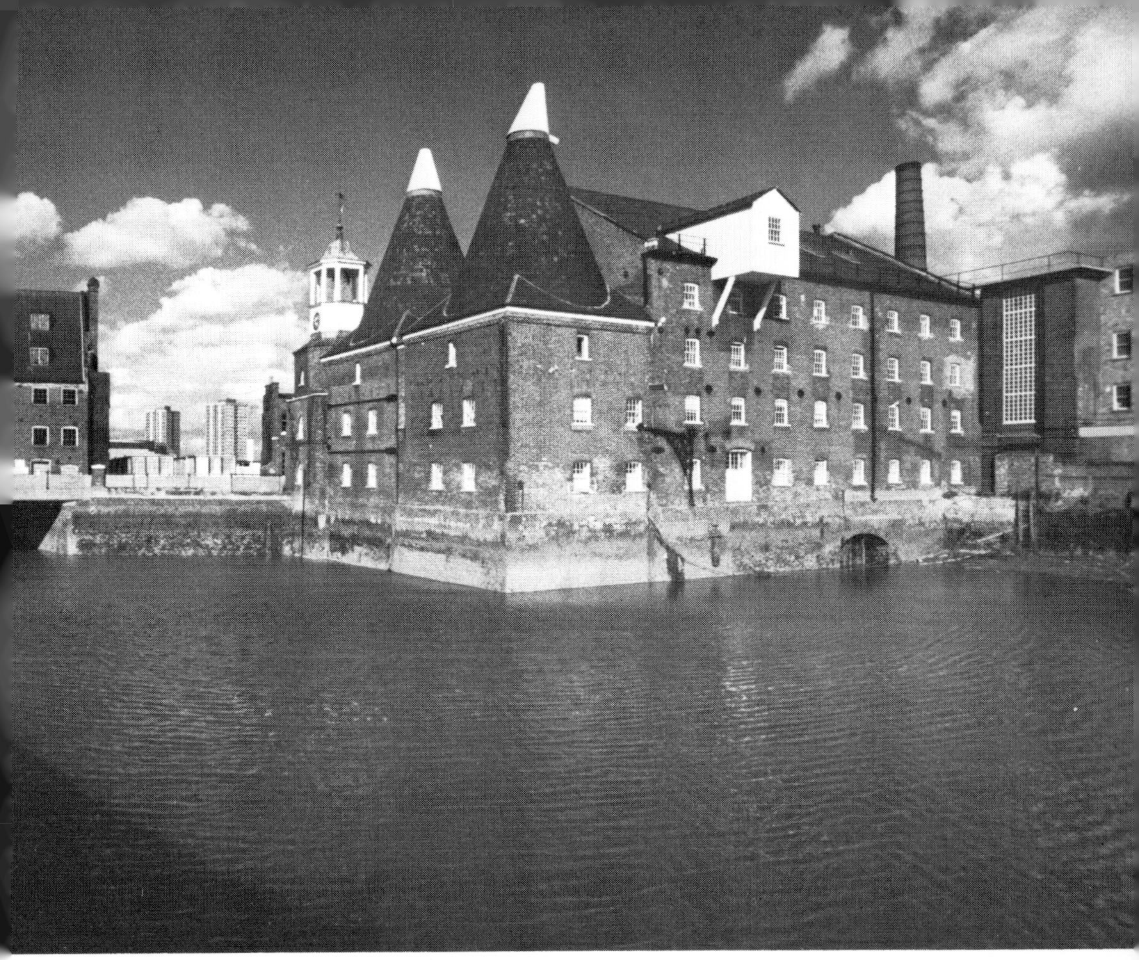

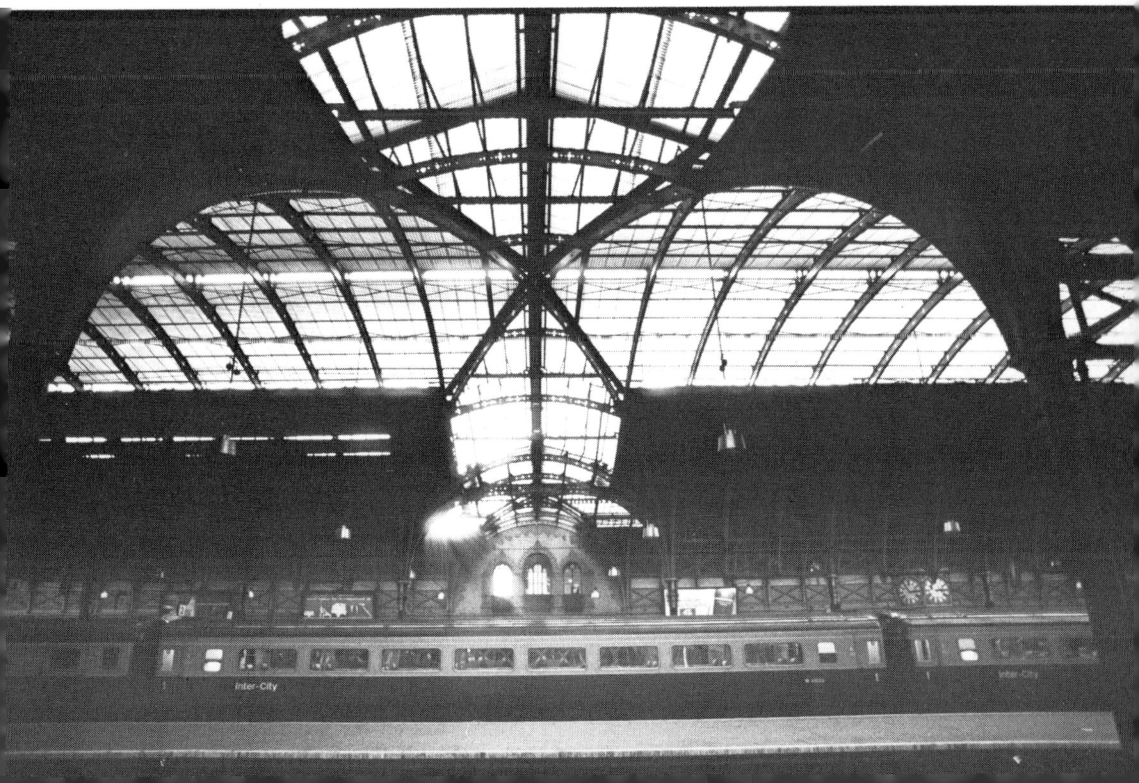
Inter-City
Inter-City

Right
Brighton station

Left
Haxted Mill, Edenbridge

Below left
Suffold Hammer Pond
bridge and sluice near
Cowfold

Below
The graceful Balcombe
viaduct on the London
to Brighton line

of the tail pole carries a fan tail and a small wheel which runs along the ground. The mill was built in about 1840 and completely restored in the 1950s, when new sweeps, tail pole and fan tail were all fitted. Sadly, when visited in 1976, one sweep had been broken off in a gale, but it is hoped that it will be restored again.

At Clayton, two mills can be seen, side by side, on the crest of the hill – Jack and Jill (TQ 304134). Jack is a tower mill, basically the same as a smock mill, but with a base of brick or masonry instead of timber, built in 1866 and Jill a little white post mill, built in 1821 and moved to the present site from Brighton. Without wishing to disparage the attractive little Clayton mills, they are really included for where they are rather than for what they are. The main interest here is in the railway, the London and Brighton. John Rennie surveyed the line, John Rastrick was chief engineer and David Mocatta the architect. Clayton tunnel says something about the abilities of all three men. It was Rennie who opted for a direct route through the Downs, which no less a man than Robert Stephenson had said was impossible; Rastrick was in charge of building the 2,259-yard tunnel; and Mocatta made sure that no one overlooked the work of his colleagues. The north portals (TQ 298141) clearly visible from the main road, were given the full Gothic treatment, including turrets, arrow slits and battlements. On top of all this grandeur is perched the rather less magnificent house where the tunnel man lived. In the early years, after the opening in 1841, the tunnel was whitewashed inside and lit by gas. Mocatta's other great contribution to the line was the splendid station at Brighton, with an engine shed that so successfully borrows the Venetian style that it would not be out of place beside the Grand Canal itself.

Architectural interest in this line does not end with the tunnel. Balcombe Viaduct (TQ 322280), which carries the line across the Sussex Ouse, stands directly in the tradition set by John Rennie's father, the canal engineer (see pp. 29 and 107). It may not be the largest or grandest, but it is certainly the most graceful of British viaducts. Thirty-seven slender arches of brick and stone carry the line a hundred feet above the river. It is a structure where the fashionable classical detailing is matched by perfect proportioning – thank heavens they had the sense not to repeat the Clayton Gothic here. Indeed, one of the virtues of Mocatta's design work was his ability to change his style with changing circumstances. There was no blinkered dogmatism here.

Across the county border in Kent, we are back with another exceptionally fine smock mill. Union Mill, Cranbrook (TQ 779359) is unusual in being set not in open country but near the centre of the little town. Seventy-two feet high, it dominates the skyline, standing high over the roof tops. Built in 1814 by James Humphrey, it has a white painted weather-boarded body above a base of tarred brick. There are four patent sails and, although it no longer relies on wind power, it is still a working mill.

Although this is an area where the windmill predominates, one watermill deserves a special mention. Haxted Mill, Edenbridge (TQ 418455) is a plain, simple structure which has much of its machinery intact, though the wheel itself is not original. It is now being developed as a museum of milling, specializing in the machinery of the watermill. Interesting now, it should become more interesting with the passing years.

The watermill could, of course, easily be adapted for grinding other materials besides grain. At Faversham (TR 009613), a grinding mill formed part of the Royal Gunpowder Factory. Few of these buildings survive, it being in the nature of the beast to disappear suddenly rather than to decay gradually – gunpowder factories were assuredly not among the safer places to look for a job. The main building material is a flimsy boarding, deliberately chosen to cause the minimum damage if an explosion did occur. Once there were four mills and two water wheels, but now only one breast-shot wheel remains, and only one of the pair of mills it powered still stands. The arrangement of wallower and spur wheel is conventional, but here the actual grinding was by edge roller. The upper stones rotated in a vertical plane to crush the raw material on the base stone. The site has been well restored.

London owes much of its interest to the industrial archaeologist to its role as the commercial heart of the country. It is, and was, the great centre of communications. There the main railway lines have their great termini; docks and warehouses line the Thames, which has always been the main factor in the city's development, but over the years the emphasis has shifted, as larger craft and more sophisticated cargo handling techniques have resulted in a steady movement away from the city centre towards the deeper, wider waters of the estuary. The older docks around the Pool no longer have any great commercial traffic, and are either being filled in or adapted to other uses. This

The South and the East

is not too surprising, since one can hardly expect a dock area built to handle the sailing ships of the 1800s to cope with the container vessels of the twentieth century. But if the usefulness of the old docks has diminished, their interest has not. These areas – the Regent's Canal Dock at Limehouse, opened in 1820, the West India (1802) and East India (1806), names that recall the days of the great Far East trade, the Royal Victoria (1855) and the Royal Albert (1880) – are surrounded by the tall, grey blocks of warehouses. The plain façades are enlivened by the horizontal rows of windows and the strong verticals of the loading bays and hoists. Undoubtedly, the outstanding example of an early dock complex is St Katharine's Dock, built in 1824, close by the Tower of London. Now it rests in the shadow of a later addition, Tower Bridge, itself an industrial monument of no small importance. The dock design was the work of Thomas Telford and the architect for the site was Philip Hardwick – sadly his dock offices were destroyed in the last war. Because this was a restricted site, in an area where land was always an expensive commodity, all available space had to be used to the full. So the brick warehouses were built out over the quay on Doric columns of stone and cast iron. These warehouses are exceptional in being 'designed' in the architectural sense. The rows of windows are enclosed in tall relieving arches, accentuating the vertical motif in the buildings and giving them a lightness rather than the feeling of heavy solidity common in warehouse blocks. In recent years, St Katharine's has been converted to a new function as a yachting basin, but much of the character of the old docks has been preserved.

The main line termini of London might seem to be too well known to require a mention, but often the well known gets overlooked simply because it is well known: we have seen it but not looked at it. King's Cross Station, for example, terminal of the Great Northern Railway, is easily overlooked beside its riotous neighbour, St Pancras, but it is a building of solid dignity and fundamental honesty. The designer was William Cubitt, and this building of 1852 is often spoken of as a perfect example of 'engineer's architecture'. The main station consists of two arched engine sheds, a basic construction, the outline of which is repeated in the entrance façade. There is no attempt at decoration, just these two great arches in brick with the clock, purchased at the Great Exhibition, in between. When you turn to St Pancras, next door, you inevitably concentrate first on Gilbert Scott's fantastic

46

Right
Bourn Mill, the oldest
surviving windmill
in Britain

Below
The flywheel and
governor at Stretham

confection, the Railway Hotel. Look behind that, however, at the Midland Railway's train hall and you find something less romantic but no less impressive. Here W. H. Barlow designed, in 1868, an area that was covered by a ridged roof 250-feet wide and 700-feet long, for many years by far the greatest covered area of its kind in the world. There is a happy historical connection between St Pancras and the very start of the railway age. Look at the iron supports and you will find the name Butterley Iron Works. This was the company founded a hundred years before by William Jessop, the canal engineer, and his partner Benjamin Outram, the leading figure in the development of tramways.

Euston could once rival King's Cross and St Pancras in grandeur, but the great triumphant Doric arch was destroyed to improve the image of British Rail, so we shall pass by that piece of mindless, official vandalism and turn to the Great Western terminal at Paddington. Here we can see the sort of breathtaking use of iron and glass that one associates with the Crystal Palace. Paddington was designed by Brunel with some rather Gothicky additions by Digby Wyatt – look, for example, at the arched office windows high over the platform. But it is the method of construction that gives it its special character. The plan has double transepts, which were built for a practical purpose, as the transverse aisles were used for traversing gear. That purpose no longer applies, but we can still admire the complex pattern of columns and arches that make Paddington train hall one of the glories of the railway system and, one could add, one of the glories of British architecture. Before leaving the subject of London's railways, there is one last building to be mentioned, the circular engine shed at Camden Town. The Round House is now a theatre, but the basic structure with its cast iron columns and domed roof is unchanged.

London has its surprises for the industrial archaeologist. It is not, for example, an area where one might expect to find evidence of the old domestic system of working. Yet in Spitalfields that evidence is to be found at every hand. This was one of the centres of the silk-weaving industry, and the merchants' houses all had garrets where the weavers worked at their hand looms. They are still there, the rather handsome eighteenth-century terraces with the long rows of weavers' windows clearly visible at the very tops of the houses. At the lower level are all the hallmarks of the period: the tall windows, the elaborate tracery of fanlights over panelled doors, the feeling for proportion. The working parts tend to be tucked away behind balustrading, like poor relations kept out of public view. The best examples are to be found in the area near Spitalfields Market, in Fournier Street and Wilkes Street and, best of all, in Puma Court, a tiny enclave with the sort of period charm more usually associated with Hampstead or Chelsea.

Another centre of eighteenth-century industrial buildings is to be found in an even less likely setting, close to the new flyover in Bow. Three Mills Lane – an enticing name – no longer leads to three mills, but it does lead to two, and very fine buildings they are. The older of the two is a tide mill, that used the tidal flow up Bow Creek and the River Lea. It is a plain, three-storey building, straddling the water. An ornate plaque dates it at 1776. The second building, of 1813, once housed a distillery and retains it alcoholic connections as it now belongs to the vintners, Hedges and Butler. It is a handsome building, which has the characteristic pyramid roof and kiln vent. It also boasts a pleasantly ornate little cupola. It was sited to take advantage of both road and river traffic: on the river side there is a weather-boarded hoist cover and an elaborate iron hoist.

Some way up the river at Kew (TQ 187780), the pumping station contains two of the grandest, and certainly the largest, Cornish engines in Britain. In 1845, the Copperhouse Foundry produced a 90-inch cylinder engine which, when it started work in 1846, was the largest of its type in the world. The beam was light for such a big engine – a mere 24 tons. Then, in 1869, it was joined by an even larger engine. The new engine was built by Harveys of Hayle with a huge 100-inch cylinder. These are grand engines, but perhaps even more interesting is another, more modestly sized engine. This is a 70-inch Bull engine, again supplied by Harveys. This type of engine was first built by Edward Bull in 1771. Instead of the familiar rocking beam, the cylinder was inverted over the shaft and the piston rod was attached direct to the pumping rods. It made for a more compact engine, but a less efficient one, and the wear and tear caused by the extra vibration in the piston rod was considerable. Kew's working days are over, but it has now joined the ranks of such stations that are open to the public.

North of London, on the far side of the Chilterns, stands Pitstone Mill (SP 945157), which is the oldest dated windmill in the country – the date 1627 can be found carved inside the mill. It is basically an open trestle post mill, mounted on a much patched circular brick base, which carries the date of some later changes, 1895. In fact, the mill has been considerably altered over the years, and has recently been restored. A good deal of the interior work is, however, original and one can only admire the quality of the craftsmanship shown in such features as the beautifully turned wooden main post.

Neighbouring Oxfordshire has a good deal to offer, and pride of place must go to the southern section of the Oxford Canal between Oxford and Napton. The route was laid down by James Brindley and offers a perfect example of the contour canal – dug, as the name suggests, to follow the natural contours of the land. Later canals forced their own way through the landscape by banking and cutting, but the Oxford Canal appears to meander through the whole countryside before reaching its destination. To appreciate this method of building, one should ideally follow the whole length of the canal, but anyone wishing to see contour cutting at its most extravagant should go and stand on the little hill at Wormleighton (SP 438552), just across the county border in Warwickshire. The canal all but encircles the hill, seeming more like a moat than a transport system, a bizarre sight that perhaps owes as much to the demands of local landowners as to engineering preference. It certainly makes for strange canal travel when your destination is clearly in view – astern.

Woodstock and Blenheim are not names that one would perhaps associate with industry, but the Blenheim estate contains a most interesting little site. Maintenance was a major occupation on a big estate, so a workshop was established at Combe Mill (SP 417150) where all the basic work could be carried out. There was a smithy for metal working and a whole range of wood-working machines from saws to lathes. The main interest lies in the method of powering the mill. At one end of the building are the remains of a water wheel, from which the drive was taken to overhead shafting and from there, via belts, to the different machines. At the opposite end, geared in to the same shaft system is a 19-inch beam engine, built in 1852. The engine's main use was as an alternative source of power for drought periods. It has recently been restored and steams again, still fired by its original boiler. The mill is an attractive stone building, graced by a small bell tower.

Oxfordshire stands at the edge of the west of England woollen region, and there are still a number of mills to be seen, including the

famous Witney blanket works (SP 355103). But the finest is certainly
the Bliss tweed mill at Chipping Norton (SP 293268). It was established
in the middle of the eighteenth century, but the present somewhat
fantastical building dates from the change to steam power in 1872. It
has four storeys, with towers at either end, and the whole building
has been given a very decorative treatment, including a cornice and
balustrade at the top. But what gives it its unique appearance is the
central domed tower, from the middle of which the mill chimney
sprouts.

Not far from Bliss Mill is the village of Hook Norton and the Hook
Norton brewery (SP 349332). Built at the end of the nineteenth century,
it has scarcely changed since and even the small horizontal steam
engine is still in daily use, not as a demonstration piece for visitors
but as part of the working life of the brewery. It is instructive to see
what a variety of jobs the engine can and does perform, from powering
the sack hoist which lifts the malt sacks to the top of the tall building
to turning the pumps that lift water – liquor, in brewer's language. Inside the brewery all the different processes can be followed in sequence.
Malted barley is ground to a powder, grist, then mashed with hot
water. Hops are added and the mixture, the wort, is boiled in a large
copper. The hops are drained off, the mixture is cooled, yeast is added
and fermentation begins. Finally, the beer is cleared, casked and eventually sent out to the pubs of Oxfordshire. Externally, the building
would be somewhat plain, were it not for the timber work that covers
the sack hoist and gives the place a curious Tudor look. Hook Norton
is one brewery where traditional methods are still used, and if the plant
looks a little old-fashioned then the great justification must be that
they are producing old-fashioned beer. All conscientious industrial
archaeologists should take the opportunity of conducting their own tests
on the end product of the process they are investigating.

Finally, in this section, we can take a look at the eastern part of the
region, over in East Anglia. Not surprisingly, in this flat windy land,
we find ourselves back with windmills. Bourn Mill (TL 312580) near
Cambridge cannot be accurately dated, but is almost certainly the
oldest surviving windmill in Britain. A deed of 1653 mentions that
a mill was standing here in 1636. It is a tiny open trestle post mill
with the simple pitched roof that was typical of the medieval mill.
Internally, the machinery has all been changed many times over, but

in its outward appearance it gives us the clearest idea we can have of the medieval mill.

Saxtead Green Mill (TM 253644) is also a post mill, but there all similarity with Bourn Mill ends. This is a late eighteenth-century mill and very sophisticated. Instead of a tail pole that has to be hauled round manually, the pole is fitted with a fan tail and a wheel that runs on a metal track. Instead of the pitched roof it was built with a curved top, which gives more space inside for the brake wheel. It has been beautifully preserved, and is the finest mill of its type in the country.

The windmill also found a role in East Anglia in land reclamation and drainage. Herringfleet Mill (TM 465974), on the banks of the River Waveney, is the last survivor of the many pumping mills that once worked in this area. It is a smock mill, built in 1830, with a boat-shaped cap. It is a simple little octagonal structure clad in rather gloomy, tarred weather-boarding. It drove a 16-foot diameter scoop wheel, which is also enclosed in wood. It has a charm of its own, and inside you can still see the little settle in front of the fireplace where the engineer could rest, away from the cold east winds.

Wind power inevitably gave way to steam power. Stretham old engine (TL 516730), built in 1831, performed precisely the same job as the Herringfleet Mill. It too turned a scoop wheel, but in this case a 37-foot-diameter wheel. The engine is a 39-inch beam engine, which has an interesting starting mechanism. A lever, let into the floor of the engine house, is used to rock the 24-foot-diameter flywheel until continuous motion is achieved, at which point automatic valve operation comes into play. The rising breast which allows water to reach the wheel is moved by a rack and pinion operated from inside the house. When working full out, the wheel could move one hundred tons of water per minute. Steam was originally raised in two waggon boilers, but these were replaced by Lancashire boilers in 1878. The engine and wheel are preserved as important relics of the days of land reclamation.

Finally, in Norwich, is a quite outstanding example of a yarn mill (TG 236092). Built on the banks of the River Wensum, it is a tall narrow brick building, six storeys high with a domed tower at one end. Built in 1839 to the design of Richard Parkinson, it is now the home of Jarrold's Printing Works.

4 The Midlands

The Midlands is an area that not only lies at the heart of England, but also at the heart of the industrial revolution. Coal has been a key factor in much of the story: coal and iron together led to major developments in the iron industry, coal and clay were the basis for development in the Potteries, and it was coal that formed the main cargo on the great network of canals that spread across the Midlands in the late eighteenth century. An appropriate place to begin any study of canals is the Grand Union at Stoke Bruerne in Northamptonshire. At the top of the Stoke locks, a mill building has been converted to house the Waterways Museum (SP 740500). As important as the collection of relics inside is the site itself, a microcosm of the canal world. The top lock lies behind a superbly elegant double-arched bridge, and around it a small settlement has developed: warehouse, cottages, pub. There is also a weigh-bridge, moved to its present site from Wales, on which there sits a narrow boat from the famous Midland carrying firm of Fellows, Morton and Clayton. A short trip along the canal brings one to Blisworth tunnel, 3,056 yards long and the longest in regular use on the whole system. From there one can continue on towards Birmingham, the hub of the Midlands network.

Birmingham itself is covered by a complex tracery of canals, known collectively as the Birmingham Canal Navigations or, more commonly, the BCN. Here can be found a number of outstanding engineering features. In the 1820s, traffic was so heavy on the old meandering main line that a new line was cut through the centre of Birmingham, straight, broad and direct, often passing through deep cuttings to keep its line and level. The cutting at its deepest was over seventy feet, and there it was crossed by Galton Bridge (SP 016969), a cast iron span of 150 feet, completed in 1829, one of the great structures of the canal age, which was soon to fade before the growing strength of the railways. Today, Galton bridge has lost its traffic to a new road scheme, and

Gladstone pottery

the canal beneath it disappears into a concrete tunnel piercing the new embankment. Canal and bridge were the work of Thomas Telford, and he again turned to cast iron when he built an aqueduct to carry one of the many branches across his new main line. The Engine Arm aqueduct (SP 024889) is less impressive but more ornate than Galton bridge. The trough is supported on a series of pillars and pointed arches in the then increasingly popular Gothic style. The Engine Arm got its name from a Boulton and Watt engine that was installed in 1778 to pump water up to the old summit level of the Birmingham Canal.

The BCN offers a view of a number of industrial sites, including that of the Soho works of Boulton and Watt, of which nothing now remains. Fortunately the same is not true of Langley Maltings beside the Titford Canal (SO 995388). These nineteenth-century buildings once belonged to Banks, the brewers, and are characteristic of this type of structure. The main ranges are three-storey, brick-built, and capped by pyramidal roofs with their prominent vents. These were floor maltings, where the barley is allowed to partially germinate, before being spread, frequently turned and finally cured in the kilns.

The Dudley Canal, turning south off the Birmingham main line, is a route of considerable interest. Dudley limestone was a valuable commodity which was used as a flux in the local ironworks. The principal landowner, Lord Dudley and Ward, set going an extensive system of quarrying and canal construction. For his Castle Mill quarry he built a private canal and from the Wren's Nest quarry he built another. One of the purposes for which the Dudley Canal was built was to link these quarries into the main canal system by means of a tunnel through the limestone ridge between the two, a tunnel that would emerge in the Wren's Nest itself (SO 945916). Dudley Tunnel is a remarkable work, alternating between seemingly impossibly narrow sections and cavernous limestone workings. The tunnel was reopened in 1973. Its main line is over 3,000 yards long, and there are another 2,000 yards of branch tunnels that can be explored. Because of a lack of ventilation, no powered craft except those with electric motors can be used in the tunnel, which gives the fitter enthusiasts an opportunity to emulate the old boatmen and 'leg' the tunnel. In this method, the boat is propelled by the leggers lying on their backs and 'walking' along the tunnel side. It is, as the author can testify, an exhausting occupation. Above ground, Dudley Castle was the scene of another event of great historical importance. It was here, in 1712, that the first Newcomen engine was set to work. The overall importance of the region has been recognized by the establishment of a Black Country Museum at Dudley which, at the time of writing, is still in its infancy.

The Dudley Canal leads, via the Delph locks, to Stourbridge, where one can find one of this country's few surviving glass cones (SO 888868). At first sight, the cone could be mistaken for the more familiar pottery kiln, but it is considerably larger and more regular in shape. Its function, in fact, was very different. Where the pottery kiln is simply an oven, the cone was workshop and furnace combined. The furnace itself was in the centre of the cone, and it was here that silica and soda, together with other materials that might be needed for special glasses, were fused together. Around the furnace, stood the men who worked the molten glass, blowing it into shape or making flat glass plates by slitting the blown bubbles. Annealing hearths in the side of the cone were used to cool the molten glass slowly to avoid brittleness. Even though entrance to the cone was through open arches, it must have been a decidedly uncomfortable place to work.

Glass cones were uncomfortable, needle factories were lethal. At Redditch Forge Mill (SP 050680) all the old processes of needle manufacture can still be traced. The first view of the mill suggests a peaceful enough scene, with the picturesque beauty of its mill pond with the old water wheel set between two ranges of mellow, brick buildings. Inside, however, one finds a mass of machinery that seems to fill every inch of space. The starting-point for needle making is rough, scaly wire which has to be cleaned, smoothed and polished. The main cleaning is done in large, wooden boxes which are geared to the drive shaft from the water wheel in such a way that they are rocked violently backwards and forwards. The needles are wrapped in cloth and packed into the boxes with a lubricant and an abrasive powder, produced in the mill by grinding. From these scouring beds, the needles are taken for further polishing in rotating barrels in the barrel shop. Needles were sent on to the second building, the grinding hull, for pointing and sharpening. Here the stones spun and the metal dust flew. Lung damage was rife in the hulls, and the pointer who reached the age of thirty considered himself a lucky man. There was the added danger from breaking stones, for the stone that broke from the wheel could decapitate a man – and once did at Redditch.

The Midlands

In this part of the Midlands it is never possible to get very far from the canal system. Birmingham stands on a plateau, and a major problem facing the engineers was that of the deep descent to the lower river valleys. The older generation overcame the problem by opting for a circuitous route, but in the later days of canal building a direct route became the goal. This would involve a good deal of lock building, which can be seen at its most spectacular on the Worcester and Birmingham Canal, completed in 1815. There are fifty-eight locks in the twenty miles from the Severn to the summit level and at Tardebigge is the longest flight of locks in the country, thirty of them, culminating in a top lock 14-feet deep. Water for the flight was pumped from the Tardebigge reservoir, and the engine house for the steam engine that once performed this task still stands (SO 985685).

The older route up from the Severn is by Brindley's Staffordshire and Worcestershire Canal. This is very much one of the first generation, completed in 1772. It was, however, of great importance for it formed one of the limbs of 'the cross', which was intended as a system of canals linking the great navigable rivers, Severn, Trent, Mersey and Thames. The Staffs and Worcester joins the Trent and Mersey, completing three parts of the system. Its importance to eighteenth-century trade can be gauged by seeing what happened at the point where the canal met the Severn. Brindley chose as his junction the spot where the little River Stour joined the main stream. Before the canal came, all that stood here was one lonely inn: after its completion there was a whole new town – Stourport. Stourport is as completely a canal town as Crewe is a railway town. Commercial buildings were clustered around the wharves and basins, among which was one graceful building, the Customs House, which still survives. Traders congregated in the area and a new hotel, the Tontine, was built. Houses were needed for the new work-force and gradually the town developed around the nucleus of the basin where the sailing boats of the river discharged their cargoes to the narrow boats of the canal. With the decline of canal trade, the centre of the town shifted, leaving the area round the basin as a purely Georgian development, as interesting to the architect as to the industrial archaeologist. One point that emerges very clearly is that there was a unity of style shared between commercial and domestic buildings. The little tollhouse, for example (SO 812715) is as charming as any rural cottage.

58

Moving north into Shropshire, one reaches an area that was once rich in lead ore which, as in the Mendips, was mined as far back as Roman times. The connection with the Roman occupation was retained in the names of some of the later mines, such as Roman Gravels. There is still some evidence of Roman open-cast workings, but the main interest is in the work of the nineteenth-century miners. Of all the mines in the region, the most important was Snailbeach (SJ 373023). It was probably the richest lead mine in the whole of England. It was owned by the Marquis of Bath, and major exploitation began in the 1780s, reaching a peak in the middle of the next century, when 3,500 tons of ore were raised and smelted per year. In the 1870s, the mine was extensively modernized with new pumping engines, a new smelter and a 28-inch gauge railway that ran from Minsterley and reached all parts of the works. Today, Snailbeach has an eerie look to it, the remains surrounded by the mountains of spoil. But there is a good deal still to see, mostly dating from the last modernization period. There are a number of engine houses in various states of decay: the most modern stands in the shadow of the spoil heaps. There is a winding engine house and, best preserved, the New Engine house, built in 1856 to house a 61-inch Cornish pumping engine. In and around the area are the remains of the smelting houses, dressing sheds and the tall chimney from one of the smelting flues. Remains of the railway include the engine shed. From remains, the whole complex system can be traced: shafts followed the veins, whim engines and pumping engines followed the shafts and these in turn can be traced, via the tramways, to the different ore treatment plants. It is a fascinating area, but one to be explored with caution, for there are many unfenced shafts.

Back on the line of the Severn is an area of unique importance to the whole history of industrial development. It is sometimes referred to as the Birthplace of the Industrial Revolution, and if that phrase rather overplays its importance it is not that wide of the mark. To see the area in some sort of perspective one should start away from the river, in the steep valley of Coalbrookdale. It was here (SJ 668047), in 1709, that Abraham Darby first successfully used coke in the smelting of iron. The importance of this discovery is difficult to overestimate. Up to that time, smelters had been forced to rely on charcoal and that, in turn, had meant reliance on far from inexhaustible stocks of timber. The industrial revolution demanded iron for machines, for rails, for buildings and, thanks to Darby, the main constraint on expansion was removed.

Darby began his career in the brass works of Bristol, where he developed a technique for casting cheap, iron cooking pots. His partners were disinterested, so he bought his own works in Shropshire. The site was ideal. Here was water for power, good coking coal, iron ore and – in case his new ideas went wrong – wood for charcoal. But they did not go wrong and successive generations of Darbys developed the Coalbrookdale works. Much remains as evidence of success – the old cooking pots, iron rails and other products of the works; the old warehouse; and, as the centre of interest, the original furnace. The furnace was already old when Darby moved in. It was tapped through an arch topped by a metal beam, which was retained in later building and carries the date 1638. Over the years, the hearth was extended and later lintels carry the date 1777. It was from this hearth that coke-smelted iron first flowed. The site was well planned to take advantage of the terrain. Furnace ponds were in series, fed by the same stream, furnaces were built against the hill for easy charging and transport problems were minimized by arranging processes in a downhill progression, from coal and ore pits at the top to finished ironwork at the bottom, ready to be sent on its way to the wharf on the Severn.

The visitor following the route down to the Severn passes Rose Cottages, recently restored as examples of the houses of the Darby workers, and reaches the wharf and warehouses (SJ 668036). Then, spanning the river, he will see the structure that gave the town of Iron-bridge its name (SJ 672033). This is perhaps the most famous industrial monument in Britain, and quite deservedly so. Designed by Abraham Darby III, completed in 1781, it was the world's first iron bridge. What a way to begin! This was no tentative start, but a massive span of 100 feet, rising to 40 feet above the river. Indeed, the only sign that the designers were at all unsure about how to handle the material can be seen in the method of construction. The different iron members are slotted together like wood in a series of mortice and dovetail joints, made solid with iron wedges. But this in no way detracts from the magnificence of the achievement.

Continuing on down the river, one comes to another set of furnaces, known as the Bedlam furnaces (SJ 678033), a name probably bestowed by visitors, viewing with alarm, as did the poetess Anna Seward, 'the red and countless fires' and 'the columns large of thick, sulpherous smoke'. Moving on again brings you to the Coalport Pottery (SJ 095025), famous in the Victorian age as the producer of elaborate, richly decorated ware. Much of the original building remains, including two old bottle kilns, one of which has been incorporated into a museum. The works straddle the small 'tub boat' canal. The main part of the canal was high up the hillside and the tubs, which, as their name suggests, were simply plain metal boxes, were floated onto wheeled bogies and then lowered down on a railed track, the Hay Inclined Plane. Like so much else in this region, the plane has been restored and the rails set back in place.

At the top of the incline is the 42-acre site of the Blists Hill Open Air Museum. This is based on existing industrial features. Pride of place must go to the furnaces and the huge vertical blowing engine that once provided the blast. There is so much here that it is difficult to decide how much to include, particularly as change is continuous and any account is soon overtaken by events. So here I shall just mention a few of the exhibits that I particularly enjoy. There is a little steam winding engine, originally used in the nearby clay pits, now in steam again, winding corves up and down the colliery shaft. There is a section of road, built by the methods laid down by Telford. Beside it stands a toll house that once stood on the Holyhead Road, and which has been restored with such loving care that to walk inside seems an invasion of privacy. There is a nineteenth-century print shop, a pottery and, at the entrance, a magnificent pair of beam blowing-engines, *David* and *Sampson*, built by Murdoch Aitken of Glasgow in 1851. Hopefully this woefully inadequate catalogue will at least indicate something of the rich variety to be found at Blists Hill.

After the completion of the Darby bridge, iron was put to other new uses. In 1795, Thomas Telford was appointed chief engineer on the Shrewsbury Canal on the death of the former engineer, Josiah Clowes. Work had already begun on a masonry aqueduct to cross the River Tern at Longdon. Telford discussed the project with one of the promoters of the canal, the ironmaster William Reynolds, and they decided to use iron for the trough instead. The canal has gone but the aqueduct remains (SJ 617157), an ungainly structure but an effective one. The iron trough had the advantage that it could be made much lighter than the old style of clay-lined masonry, and so supports could also be lighter. Here the trough is carried on triangulated iron supports, with extra vertical supports for the towpath which was next to the main trough. Longdon was the trial, and Telford left the Shrewsbury Canal to go back to work as assistant to William Jessop on the Ellesmere Canal. There he put his experience with ironwork to spectacular use (see p. 144).

Shropshire can certainly claim its fair share of iron 'firsts'. Ditherington Mill (SJ 499139) is the first iron-framed factory. Early factories, like early mills, were generally constructed on the basis of wooden pillars and beams, with the result that they represented a considerable fire risk. In 1796, Charles Bage of Benyon, Benyon and Bage designed this building as a flax mill, using a series of iron columns to support brick jack arches. The building is now used by Allied Breweries, but its original function can easily be detected from the many windows, now bricked in, and from the way in which the central row of columns was designed with holes to take the overhead drive shaft.

By early nineteenth century, the use of iron as a construction material was commonplace, and engineers were already beginning to appreciate the savings that could be made by using standardized components. When Telford returned to the Shropshire area in 1825 as chief engineer for the Birmingham and Liverpool Junction Canal, he again used cast iron for his aqueducts, and used the same basic castings for each of them. However, where the canal crossed the road at Stretton (SJ 872108), something special was obviously called for, as this was a Telford canal crossing a Telford road. The Holyhead Road (A5) perhaps represents Telford's greatest achievement in civil engineering, though the Birmingham and Liverpool runs it a close second. The conjunction of the two was celebrated at the aqueduct, which has finely dressed circular stone pillars at either end and has an inscription cast into the centre panel of the ironwork – though few of the hurrying motorists now look up and see it. Interestingly, the same basic casting can be seen on the Macclesfield Canal as well.

Aqueducts are not the main interest on the Liverpool and Birmingham, now better known as the Shropshire Union main line. The southern Oxford is a perfect example of an early canal – here is the late canal. Where the one meandered, this heads straight for its destination. A quite different engineering technique was used – cut and fill. Hills were pierced by deep cuttings and the spoil from the cuttings was used to build up embankments across the valleys. The deep cuttings are the more spectacular, man-made ravines, overhung with vegetation. One of the most impressive is Woodseaves, where the navvies have left the marks of pick and drill on the solid rock walls. The cutting is straddled by a tall, high-arched bridge (sj 688308), of the type usually known as 'rocket bridges', from the sweeping curve of the abutments. The banks, though offering less visual excitement, offered excitement enough to the engineers. Shelmore embankment (sj 803215 to sj 793227) collapsed several times during the construction, so that work on it had to continue for more than five years. Stop locks can still be seen at either end, ready to isolate the section in an emergency.

Further south, the canal passes through the grounds of Chillington Hall, so the company obligingly produced a suitably grand, balustraded bridge to carry the avenue over the canal (sj 889076). This was not an uncommon practice on the canals, but was something of a rarity on the railways. But across in Staffordshire, the engineers of the Trent Valley Railway were faced with a similar situation when they wished to cross the Lichfield Drive into Shugborough Park (sj 998212). The bridge that carries the line across the drive is far grander than its canal equivalent. It has the same classical approach with balustrading and pairs of ionic columns, but plinths have been added to carry the figures of lion and horse, the supporters of the Anson arms, while the arms themselves are raised on a tall central plinth. It is an architectural curiosity – grandiose rather than grand – but it has a historical significance as a reminder of the often lengthy battles waged between railway companies and landowners before tracks could be laid.

The Trent and Mersey Canal also runs past Shugborough Park. This is the canal built largely to meet the needs of the industrialists of Stoke-on-Trent. The city of Stoke is a conglomerate made up of six – not five – towns, and is the heart of the potteries. Before looking at that industry in more detail, we shall conclude the survey of transport in the area. The main feature on the canal is the Harecastle tunnel or, to be more precise, tunnels. The original was begun by Brindley in 1766, but was not completed until 1777, after his death. It was the first major canal tunnel in the country, 2,879 yards long, but uncomfortably narrow, and a second tunnel was built alongside it by Telford. This came complete with the luxury of a towpath. The north portal at Kidsgrove (SJ 840540) is the more accessible. The North Staffordshire Railway came to challenge the canals in the 1840s. Stoke was their headquarters, so it was only fitting that Stoke should be given a suitably imposing station. Where other lines went in for Classical or Gothic styles, the North Staffordshire opted for Jacobean. Stoke Station (SJ 879456) has a magnificent façade, with shaped gables rising above a front marked by a huge bay window that would not have disgraced the finest manor. It could all be mildly absurd, but it is carried through with such panache as to defy criticism.

The name that dominates the eighteenth-century history of the Potteries is that of Josiah Wedgwood. It is an oversimplification, but nevertheless largely true, to say that it was through his example and influence that Staffordshire pottery moved from being a craft-based industry, serving largely local requirements, to a mass-production industry serving the world. He was the chief promotor of the Trent and Mersey Canal, which enabled the potters to bring in bulk raw material, such as china clay from the West Country and to send out their finished ware to the ports. He changed the basis of industrial production, first by applying scientific experimental techniques to industrial production – systematically experimenting and meticulously recording results. It was by pursuing these methods that he was able to produce his cream-coloured earthenware, later christened Queen's ware, which was the basis of his success and the green and blue Jasper ware with which the name Wedgwood is still associated. His partner, Thomas Bentley, was the brilliant entrepreneur who ensured that the ware was bought. Wedgwood's main contribution to the potteries lay in his successful revolution in the methods of production. Before his time, the pottery worker was the journeyman-craftsman, able to turn his hand to any requirement of the trade. Wedgwood built a new kind of pot factory, one where process followed process in logical sequence through the works, with each department staffed by specialists.

Not much remains that links directly back to Wedgwood. There is the Midland Bank in Swan Square, Burslem, once known as the Big House, which was built in 1751 by Thomas and James Wedgwood, relations who leased Josiah his first pot works. The most important site is Etruria. It was here, beside the Trent and Mersey Canal, that Wedgwood opened his revolutionary new factory in 1769. Sadly, the site was levelled in 1968 and all that now stands is a small, circular building with a domed roof that once stood at the end of the main range of buildings (SJ 869473). It is said to have been a modelling shop, but its shape is no clue to its use as it was only built that way in order to preserve symmetry, balancing a bottle kiln at the opposite end. Etruria was more than just a factory, for Wedgwood built a village round the works, some cottages of which still stand, and his own home, Etruria Hall, which still faces the site from across the water.

Though there are scant remains of Wedgwood's works, his influence can still be seen throughout the region. The classical style he adopted for the works at Etruria became the norm for the whole industry. The Aynsley China works in Sutherland Road, Longton, for example (SJ 914433) shows all the main characteristics. The façade is regular, three storeys high, with a dentilled cornice. The only access to the central courtyard around which the different sections are grouped is via a central opening under a flat elliptical arch. The central block is the focal point of the building. Above the arch is a Venetian window, above that a three-light window, with the lights divided by columns and over them all is a pediment. The arrangement of the works is practical, the decoration Classical, suited to the type of ware that made Wedgwood and his contemporaries famous. This same basic design can be found repeated over and over again throughout the district, though there are minor variations. An exception to the single entrance rule can be found in some works which have a special 'hole in the wall' through which clay was tipped, as for example in Lawley Street, Longton (SJ 918430), where the brickwork around the hole is whitened by the clay. What one can rarely see any longer is a complete works in the old style. The façade might remain, but behind it there has usually been sweeping change. The exception is the Gladstone Pottery in Uttoxeter Road, Longton (SJ 912433). The works have been preserved as an industrial museum, and the whole manufacturing process of a nineteenth-century pot works can be seen.

The pottery has changed little since the 1850s. Buildings are grouped around a courtyard, the only access to which is through the tunnel entrance. The main offices were built above, so that management could keep all the comings and goings in sight. Clay and other raw materials were dumped in the courtyard, before being taken to the mixing house where they were mixed in a vat, stirred by a propellor turned by a small steam engine. The clay was then either dried for throwing or left wet for casting, and it began its tour of the works. In the different departments it was cast, moulded and shaped until it had the required form. The ware was then placed in saggars, fire-proof containers which were loaded into the first of the bottle ovens, the biscuit oven. It was here that the basic ware was fired. After that decoration could be added – glaze, printed illustrations, painting or gilding – and the ware refired in the appropriate oven. At first sight, a pot works is an incoherent jumble of buildings, but in fact the sequence is a logical one, with the basic business of producing glazed pots occupying the ground floor of the different workshops, while the upper storeys contained the workshops where decoration and other fine work was done under the skylights which gave good, even illumination.

A number of subsidiary industrial buildings can be found in the Potteries, of which the most common are the grinding mills. Here essential raw materials – flint for whitening the clay body, bone for bone china and colouring matter – were ground for the potters. The Etruscan Bone and Flint Mill (SJ 872468) stands beside the Trent and Mersey Canal on the Etruria flight, close to the junction with the Caldon Canal – emphasizing again the importance of the canal for bulk transport. The mill was steam powered, and the old gabled engine house still stands, dated by a plaque on the wall at 1857. Beside it, the main range extends along the arm of the canal to end in the squat, pyramidal chimney of the kilns. An earlier flint mill, in what is virtually a perfect state of preservation, can be found by following the Caldon Canal to Cheddleton (SJ 972528). Here, it is claimed, the canal's engineer, James Brindley, temporarily doffed his canal hat and replaced it with his old millwright's headgear. Whether the machinery at Cheddleton is actually the work of Brindley is open to question.

The process at Cheddleton begins at the wharf. Here flints were unloaded from the boats and heated in kilns built into the wharf itself. Heat made the flints brittle and from the kilns they were taken on a short tramway to one or other of the two mill buildings. These are each powered by wheels turned by water from the River Churnet. In the north mill, extensively modified in the late eighteenth century, the flints were taken to the first floor, placed in grinding pans, mixed with water and crushed under stones set into the circling sweep arms. The resulting slurry was run off into settling arcs and the powdered flint

66

finally dried, originally in sun pans, later in a drying kiln. The south mill is similar, but considerably older, and has an ingenious water-powered beam pump that was used to lift the water up to the grinding pan. The length of stroke of the pump could be altered by moving the pivotal point along the beam.

The flint mills have pride of place at Cheddleton, but the immediate area has a number of interesting features. Beside the canal stands a long building which has served a number of different functions over the years. In the early nineteenth century, steam power was brought in and it became a silk factory, where silk was both spun and woven. On the far side of the bridge carrying the Leek turnpike road are large lime kilns and a slipway for a boatyard.

In Leek, we can follow up two of the themes begun at Cheddleton. There may be doubts about Brindley's responsibility for the flint mills, but there is no doubt that he designed the machinery for Leek corn mill (SJ 977570). It is an elegant little building, with arched windows and a bull's eye window over the main door. Power came from a 16-foot-diameter undershot water wheel and was transmitted through the usual system of pit wheel and wallower to the 10-foot-diameter spur wheel, from which the stone nuts and hence the stones are driven. A pinion and pulley system also meshes with the spur wheel to work the sack hoist. It would be a good example of a conventional corn mill, even if it had no associations with the famous. There is one memento of the great man – the initials JB and the date 1752 are carved by a first floor window.

The principal industry in Leek was silk, and the finest surviving example of an early silk mill is unquestionably Albion Mill (SJ 983561). Built in 1815, it is a plain enough building, three storeys high with a hipped roof and a little bell tower. Though the design is plain, the effect created in the building is quite gaudy because of the two-coloured chequered brickwork. The mill was steam powered and the boiler house stands at the end of the factory. Even after this and other mills were built, silk weaving continued as a domestic industry and around the corner, in King Street, a whole row of weavers' houses can be seen. They have the same chequered brickwork as the mill and top floor workshops.

Silk manufacture was concentrated around the Leek-Macclesfield area, but in the south-eastern part of the country, the main textile production was in cotton. The region was among the very first to use the new spinning machinery, and one of the principal manufacturers was Robert Peel, father of Robert Peel the politician. One of his mills was built at Fazeley in 1795, a typical, plain three-storey building, originally water powered and much extended in later years (SK 203016). The area continued to prosper and more mills were added. It is interesting to compare the later buildings with the earlier. Close by Peel's Mill, on the bank of the Birmingham and Fazeley Canal, stands a mill of 1883. By then, the steam mill had been standardized, and this rather gaunt five-storey building, with its tall stack, is all but indistinguishable from scores of its contemporaries. It is purely functional with no trimmings.

A curiosity of the textile world can be found to the south in Coventry. Here, in 1857, Joseph Cash, built his Top Shops (SP 335805). These consisted of rows of houses, originally forty-eight in all, above which a continuous workshop was placed. To start the day, Cash's workers would pop up through trap doors to work at the looms. It was a kind of halfway house between the domestic and the factory system. Power for the looms came from a steam engine in the courtyard. This has gone, but its tall, ornate stack remains. The top shops themselves are now used as storage space and weavers still work, producing name tapes, down in the courtyard.

Over in Leicester, development in the textile industry was rather more widespread. This was an area especially noted for its connections with the hosiery industry (see p. 76), and it was natural to consider placing spinning factories in a region which had so many potential users of the end product. Architecturally, the most interesting of the old mills, since the demolition of most of the extravagent Gothic Bow Bridge Mill, is the Donisthorpe factory in Bath Lane, which backs onto the Grand Union Canal (SK 580045). It has been much extended over the years, but the central brick section, with its hipped roof, cupola and weather vane is unmistakably eighteenth century. The ram motif which the company adopted, which can be seen on the name plate by the main entrance and on the weather vane, has led to some speculation that wool was also spun here, but there is no doubt that cotton predominated.

Leicester has recently opened an industrial museum, based on the Abbey Park sewage pumping station, which might not sound the most romantic of settings. But the Victorians regarded such matters with a very proper seriousness: good sewage treatment was a civic benefit, and they saw no reason why a pumping station should not be given a certain grandeur. The work was done by four compound beam engines, each with a 4-foot-diameter low-pressure cylinder and a 30-inch high-pressure cylinder. The beams are 29-feet long. These massive engines were built in 1891 and were set to work in splendid surroundings. The main structural supports are cast iron columns with foliated capitals and the walls are decorated with red and white tiles. The cylinders of the engines are encased in wood and bound in brass, and brass gleams on all the instruments and gauges. The old boiler house contains a number of exhibits. There is transport for the living, in the form of a horse tram and for the dead in the shape of a sombrely magnificent hearse. There is also a good collection of knitting machines. Outside is a huge Ruston-Bucyrus steam shovel, which was supplied to the Alpha Cement Works at Kidlington, Oxfordshire in 1935. Both this and the beam engines are steamed from time to time.

Staffordshire, Leicestershire and neighbouring Nottinghamshire are among the major centres of coal production, and there are a number of sites which demonstrate different aspects of the industry. The colliery village often has a quite distinctive character – a small community, dominated by the colliery which would employ the whole of the local work force. Alvercote, near Tamworth, is typical of the old style of village. It is a linear village, consisting of a main street bordered on one side by the railway and the canal and on the other by the long terraces of miners' houses. Behind them, the spoil heaps rear up and the mining flashes, artificial lakes formed by subsidence, dot the landscape.

Because mining is an industry where successive generations work on the same site, the new necessarily comes in at the expense of the old. Sometimes, a structure is dismantled and re-erected on another site. At one time, a horse gin was in use at Pixton Green Colliery on the Nottingham–Derbyshire border. It was one of many such devices which were once to be seen at collieries throughout the land. It consisted of a stout wooden frame which held a wooden drum mounted on a vertical pole. The drum was turned by a horse harnessed to a horizontal shaft attached to the drum. As the horse plodded round a circular track, so rope was wound or unwound on the drum, raising

Left
The Engine Arm aqueduct
carrying a branch arm
across the Birmingham
Canal

Right
Stourbridge glass cone

Far right
Coalport Pottery

Left
The Hay Incline –
tubs floated off
their bogies when they
reached the bottom

Right
Inside Telford's
Harecastle tunnel

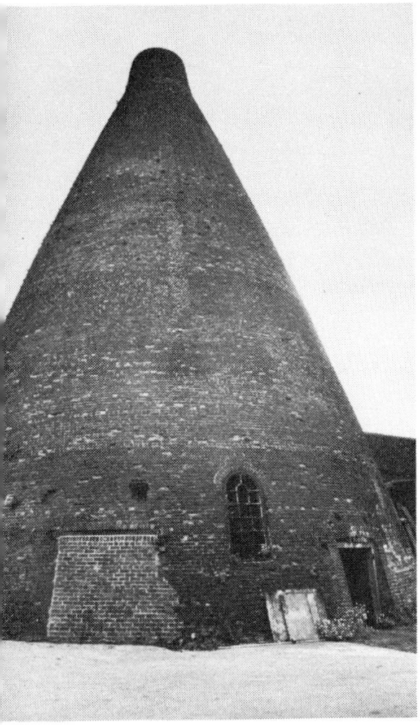

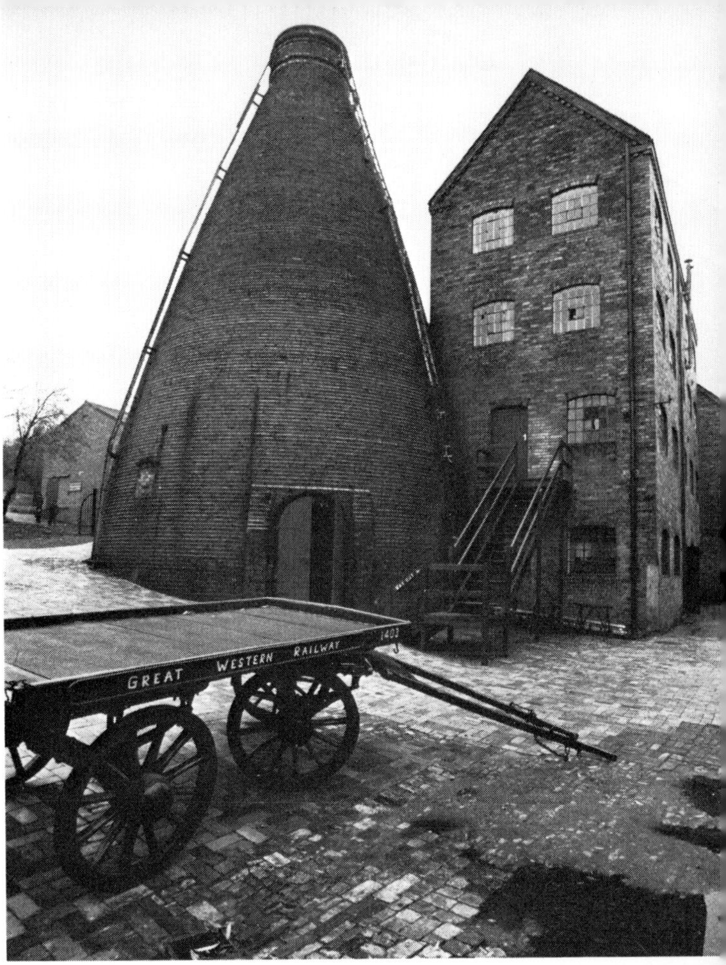
GREAT WESTERN RAILWAY
1403

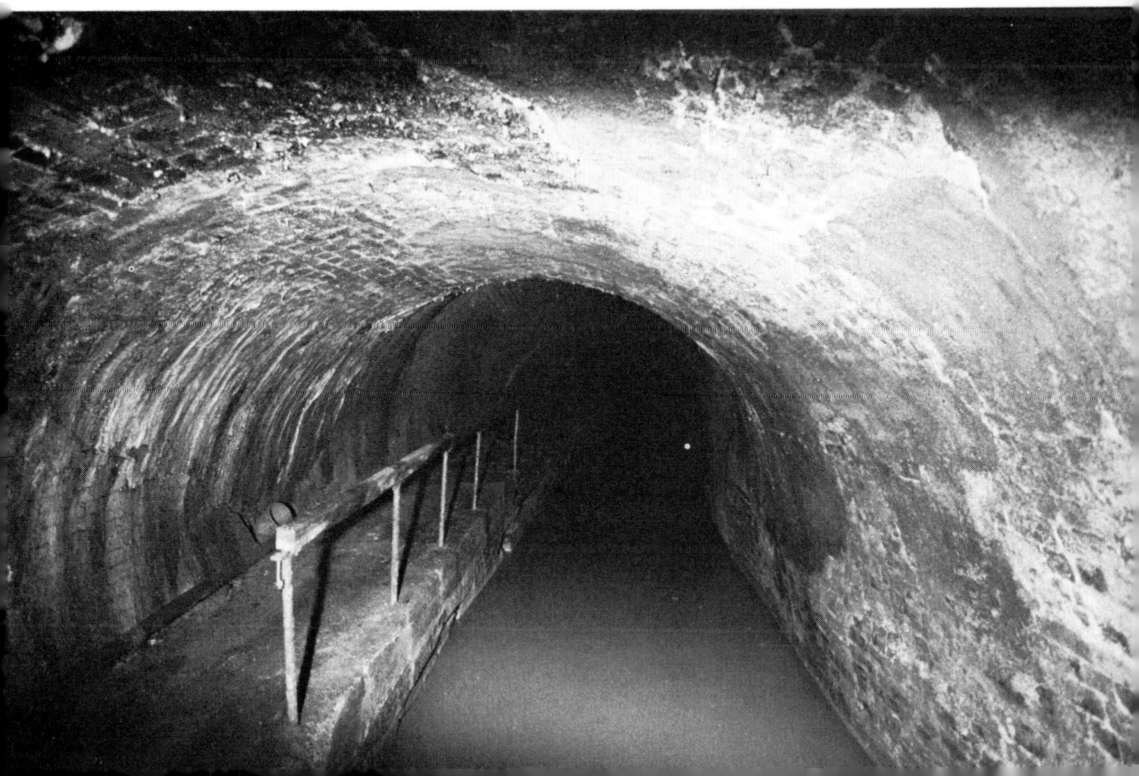

Above
The Etruscan Bone and
Flint Mill beside the
Trent and Mersey Canal

Left
Arkwright's Mill at
Matlock Bath, enlarged
when the steam power
was brought in

Right
Pressure gauges and
flywheel at Abbey Lane
pumping station, Leicester

Left
The remains of one of
the blast furnaces at
Morley Park ironworks

Right
The engine house at the
top of Middleton Incline
on the High Peak railway;
the pulley was part of
the haulage system

Below
Vertical winding engine
at Beeston colliery

or lowering material in the shaft. Pixton Green was the last gin to survive in the area, and it has now been restored and re-erected in the courtyard of the Wollaton Hall museum (SK 522392). Inside the museum are a number of exhibits connected with the local industries of lace and hosiery manufacture.

The Pixton Green gin had a long life because it was conveniently slow for shaft inspection, but in most collieries the horse gin was soon replaced by the steam engine. At Bestwood Colliery (SK 557478), one of the rare vertical winding engines, built in 1873, has been preserved and is scheduled for restoration. The engine house is a narrow, three-storey building and an unusual feature of the site is the presence of the original headstock and winding gear above the shaft.

Nottingham is famous for its lace manufacture. Lace-making was originally a domestic industry, but by the 1820s the movement towards mechanization and the factory was gaining momentum. The factories themselves are mostly disappointingly drab buildings, with the notable exception of the Anglo-Scotian mill in Wollaton Road, Beeston (SK 5336). Built in the 1870s, it is basically no more than a conventional four-storey, red brick mill with an attic and rows of segmented arched windows, but the builders have stuck a Gothic façade on the front, with lancet windows, crenellated towers and parapet.

To the north of Nottingham is what must surely be the most ornate industrial building in Britain, Papplewick pumping station (SK 582522). It was built in 1884 to supply water for the Nottingham district. From the outside it has a mildly gloomy Gothic air, but inside is a temple of steam. The whole installation cost £51,000, of which £11,500 went on the two 46-inch beam engines, which were among the last ever built by James Watt and Co. of Birmingham, and a good deal of the rest went on furbishing the engine house. All the decoration has a watery motif. The supporting iron columns are rich with decoration – bright-work fishes swim up and down, while the capitals are graced with ibises and lilies. Stained glass windows continue the theme, each one showing some different water plant. What an extraordinary building this is when you consider that until recently all this splendour was seen by none but the few workmen who tended the engines. You can see precisely how much work these engines were required to do, for outside is a complete set of pump rods, the whole 210 feet of them that were needed to reach the underground reservoir. Papplewick is an appropriate place for a steam temple, for it was here in 1785 that the Robinsons introduced the first ever steam engine to be used to power a cotton mill. It was a Boulton and Watt engine, but nothing now remains of engine or engine house, though some traces of the Robinson concern can be seen at Castle Mill (SK 545510) and Grange Farm (SK 547502).

Not far away is the village of Calverton. This was the home of the Rev. William Lee, the inventor of the knitting frame, who built the first machine in 1589. The basic action of pushing threads through loops was performed by a series of hooks that could be opened and closed. The machine was designed for making hose and was held in a stout wooden frame, from which its popular name of stocking frame derives. It was operated by one man, using both hands and foot treadle. The trade was originally centred in London, but in the middle of the eighteenth century it came back to the Midlands. Framework knitting was a largely domestic industry and gave rise to a distinctive style of house, the knitter's cottage. A number can be seen at Calverton, the best being Windles Square (SK 6149). The ground floor workshops are marked by long, many-paned windows that threw light onto the frame. There were also employers who grouped knitters together in special workshops and at the end of the main road in Calverton is the two-storey Dovey shop. Like the houses, it has rows of long windows. One of the Calverton cottages has been converted into a small museum.

In the north eastern part of the region one comes to the flat, rich agricultural land of Lincolnshire. Like Norfolk and Suffolk, it is an area notable for land drainage schemes and windmills. At Heckington (TF 145437) is the only surviving eight-sailed mill in the country. A tower mill, built in 1830, it has been fully restored. Further east is the once thriving port of Boston. The Witham silted up in the late eighteenth century, so that the port could no longer be used by large vessels. The warehouses of that period were therefore never replaced and still stand (TF 3343), providing a perfect example of an eighteenth-century dock frontage. They are mostly plain brick buildings, but are often redeemed from mere dullness by the use of arched windows. The Customs warehouse is particularly fine, having the more elaborate doors and windows to match its official importance.

Another eighteenth-century port, but this time inland, is to be seen at Shardlow, near the junction of the Trent Navigation and the Trent and Mersey Canal. Like Stourport, it was a canal new town, but on a much smaller scale. In the past decade, much of old Shardlow has been demolished, but enough remains to make it well worth a visit. Shardlow Basin (SK 444304) has some fine Georgian buildings, including warehouses, pubs and houses. The former are often the most decorative, including such details as a rounded waggon corner above which the first floor is carried out on a corbel, and attractive little semi-circular windows. The outstanding building is the Trent Corn Mill, built of brick in 1780, with a large arched loading bay under which the narrow boats could be floated.

Derbyshire is a county that no longer carries very strong industrial associations, but this was very far from being the case in the eighteenth century when it saw some momentous changes. Some of these early sites have simply been abandoned, left as lonely relics, and none is lonelier than the iron-making site of Morley Park (SK 380492), near Hege. Four hundred men were once employed here and now all that is left is a pair of furnaces, like truncated pyramids, in the middle of a wide expanse of fields. The furnaces stand more than 30 feet high, built into the slope to allow easy charging from the top. They are constructed from local sandstone, with the stronger gritstone to reinforce the quoins and arches. They are dated above the hearths at 1780 and 1818.

The most important event in the history of the county was unquestionably the foundation by Richard Arkwright of the world's first water-powered cotton spinning mill. He had already experimented with machinery for cotton spinning in Nottingham, where he used horses for power, and the experiments were sufficiently successful for him to begin a new mill with his partners, Jebediah Strutt and Samuel Need. He chose the hamlet of Cromford, conveniently set on the banks of the Derwent and conveniently far from any traditional textile area where he might expect to find violent opposition to his factory. (A wise precaution: when he later tried to establish a mill in Lancashire it was burned down.) So Cromford was chosen and became the first of the cotton towns. The mill itself (SK 298569) has been much altered over the years since work first started in 1771. Some parts have gone and there have been numerous additions. Originally it was a tall, narrow building, and the general shape can be seen from the remaining sections. Inside, was Arkwright's newly invented spinning machinery, the water frame, so called because water was used for power. The machines were simple. The cotton was stretched by being passed through rollers moving at different speeds then picked up by a 'flier', a rotating metal arm which imparted the twist. The mill may have changed, but much of Cromford remains the same. In North Street, one can see the houses that Arkwright built for the work force that he recruited from the Poor Houses of Britain. Solid and robust rather than elegant, they are built to a far higher standard than anything provided in the towns that were to grow up around the mills in the next century. The top floors still show the lines of weavers' windows. The mill employed mainly women and children and the menfolk were expected to provide for themselves by framework knitting. The air of solid prosperity that surrounds modern Cromford is misleading, for in Arkwright's time the life of the mill workers was hard and harsh. The owner himself, however, prospered greatly, as Willersley Castle (SK 295572), the house he built for himself testifies.

Arkwright moved on from Cromford to open up more mills. Masson Mill at Matlock Bath (SK 293572) has been extended since Arkwright's day and steam power was brought in to replace water power in the nineteenth century, but the main features of the original mill have been retained. The leat from the Derwent is still in water, and the façade shows the unmistakable characteristics of a Georgian mill. The central bay is neat and handsome, built of red brick with contrasting white stone at the quoins. Attractive Venetian windows flank the semi-circular windows above the central doorway.

The development of the textile mills in the area created a need for better transport. A canal was built and linked by a horse tramway to the Peak Forest Canal on the opposite side of the Pennine ridge. The Cromford and High Peak Railway is one of the most remarkable of all early railways, and much remains to be seen. Although it was built to the standard gauge of 4ft 8½in, the engineer still used the old technique of mounting fish-bellied rails on stone blocks. The major difficulty was, of course, the terrain and a number of inclines were built, along which the trucks were hauled by stationary steam engines. Middleton incline is topped by a polygonal engine house that still contains its old engine (SK 276552). The whole line can be traced, zig-zagging its way through the hills to the terminal at Whaley Bridge (see p. 96).

Arkwright had the reputation, which seems richly deserved, of being a difficult and boorish man. His partners clearly thought so, and Jebediah Strutt left to run his own concern at Belper. This was Strutt's town as much as Cromford was Arkwright's. Here, in North Mill (SK 345481) is an early cotton mill of quite outstanding importance. It is not merely part of the Strutt complex but also, being built in 1803, one of the earliest surviving examples of the iron-framed, fireproof mill. North Mill is an L-shaped building, six storeys high, with one wing of fifteen bays and the other of six. Starting at the basement level, one can see the huge wheel pit and the basis of the whole iron framework, thick pillars resting on pyramids built up of irregular stone blocks. The upper floors are supported on shallow brick arches that spring from beams resting on the pillars. Iron ties join the pillars, counteracting the thrust of the arches. The whole structure seems very delicate at the upper levels, but is in fact very rigid and strong. Other features of the building include a stove for central heating in the basement, and an attic with an internal gutter, a curious and rather unsatisfactory device.

As at Cromford, much of the original housing remains, including the sturdy stone terraces of Long Row and the Clusters, made up of four houses joined together in a solid square. At the opposite end of the Derwent bridge from the mill stands the cottage hospital run by Mrs Strutt, while by the mill itself is a somewhat grimmer reminder of old times. The footbridge across the main road has gun embrasures, and was built after Arkwright's Lancashire mill was burned and it was feared that the riots might spread to Derbyshire.

Other early mills can be found in the area, including one other that became the centre of a 'company town'. In 1783, Thomas Evans established mills at Darley Abbey, to the north of Derby (SK 354387). The present mill buildings, built around 1800, stand beside the extensive weir and are reached by an iron toll bridge. The town itself is of considerable interest, for development stopped here at a very early date. There are varied housing patterns, with blocks, courtyards and terraces. The community buildings include a school and, on the outskirts, the Evans farm which provided much of the food for the village.

Further north is the town of Wirksworth where Arkwright established a mill in 1783 (SK 283539). The main interest here, however, lies in the town's importance as the centre for the lead mining industry. Like other such areas, working here can be traced back to the Roman occupation and the area was heavily worked in the medieval period. A delightful reminder of that age can be found in Wirksworth church, where there is a carving, believed to date from the twelfth century, showing a miner with his pick and his kibble, the basket he used for carrying the ore. Of the mines themselves, the best preserved surface remains are those of the Magpie Mine, near Sheldon (SK 173682). There are two engine houses, looking very similar to their Cornish counterparts, which is not very surprising since they were built by Cornish engineers. The larger of the two housed the pumping engine and the smaller a whim engine, the cable drum for which is still in place. The remains include the manager's house and the small smithy, where simple maintenance work was carried out. The shafts and galleries have been extensively explored, but this is very much a job for the expert. The same is true of the soughs, the drainage tunnels, often stretching for miles, that carried the water away from the workings. Outlets can be seen in many parts, for example at Yatestop Sough (SK 263623) and Hill Carr Sough (SK 260326).

Finally there are two Derbyshire sites of special historical importance to two rather different industries. Derby was the site chosen for the installation of the first machines in Britain for throwing silk. Thomas Lombe took over an old mill building in the early 1700s, then in 1718 built a new water-powered mill specifically designed to house the new machines. The old silk mill can thus claim to be Britain's first water-powered textile factory, and though little now remains it is a site of some considerable interest. The mill was built on an island, where the foundations can be traced and the bridge that connected it to the mainland still stands (SK 345365). One cannot leave Derbyshire without a mention of Burton-on-Trent, still the biggest centre of brewing in the country and still dominated by the great breweries of the nineteenth century, even if most, like the beer they produce, are much changed. To celebrate its bicentenary in 1977, the Bass Brewery opened a brewing museum, housed in the old joiner's shop on the main site. The museum emphasizes the importance of transport, and its exhibitions include a reconstruction of a loading bay at which one of the original Bass tank locomotives stands.

5 The North

South Yorkshire means steel and coal. Sheffield is and was the focal point of a thriving industrial community, and although the centre of the city has been redeveloped, there are still a number of interesting sites to be found on the outskirts. Of these the most famous is the Abbeydale scythe works beside the River Sheaf (SK 325820). The buildings date from a variety of periods, for work began here in 1712 and changes were still being made well into the nineteenth century. But, for all that, the place has a feeling and look of unity. The buildings are grouped round a courtyard, between the river and the pond for the two wheels. The starting point for the processes at Abbeydale is not at the entrance but in the far corner of the courtyard, where steel, the material used for edging the scythes, was manufactured from iron. Here the crucible steel method, devised by Benjamin Huntsman in 1742, was used. The first stage is the manufacture of the fireproof crucibles themselves in the pot shop, where fireclay, china clay and coke dust were kneaded then shaped into tall pots. These were taken to the furnace, with its characteristic oblong stack, to be filled with carefully weighted amounts of iron and carbon and fired. The molten metal was then formed into ingots and taken to the tilt forge, where the steel was wedged between two pieces of iron then shaped and cut to form a rough scythe blade. This was achieved by beating the hot metal under tilt hammers, powered by a backshot water wheel. Water powered everything here – the hammers, the cutting shears and a two–cylinder blowing machine that provided the draught for the forge. A second wheel turned the grinding stones in the adjoining grinding hull. Individual forges were used for straightening and hardening the rough blades and the blades were bored in the boring shop to allow handles to be fitted. Also grouped around the yard are the fitting shop, warehouse, counthouse and, near the entrance, the homes of the manager and his workforce. Abbeydale was more than a factory, it was a complete industrial community.

83

Ryhope pumping station

The North

Sheffield's reputation was built not on scythes but on cutlery, and at one time the rivers of the region were lined with grinding hulls where knives were sharpened and forks pointed – and where men paid the price in damaged lungs. Typical of these small works is the Shepherd Wheel on one of the Sheaf tributaries to the east of the city (SK 317854). Power for the two workshops came from a single 18-foot overshot wheel. The long rows of windows in the hulls were very necessary, for on working days the whole space inside was dark with flying dust.

Another well preserved forge site is at Wortley on the River Don (SK 304998). As at Abbeydale, metal is shaped under water-powered hammers, but here they are built to a somewhat different design. The Abbeydale hammers are tilt hammers, where projections on a rotating wheel pick up and drop the end of the hammer. These are belly helve hammers, where the wheel acts at the halfway point along the hammer. A wooden beam on top of the hammer acts as a spring, increasing the force of the blow. This is a site with a long history, for iron was worked here from 1640 right through to the end of the nineteenth century, when it was used for making chains and railway axles – the grooved anvils where the axles were shaped can still be seen.

Coal for the forges was no problem: the area is rich in it. Only a few miles from Wortley is one of the industry's most important histori- cal monuments, the Elsecar pumping engine (SK 388999). This is one of the few remaining examples of a Newcomen-type atmospheric engine, and it still stands on the site where it spent its working life. Engine and engine house were built at the end of the eighteenth century, and though the lintel is dated at 1787, it seems more likely that it was not in use until 1795. In many ways, the Elsecar engine is similar to other beam engines, with half of the beam, carrying the pump rods, projecting out from the top of the engine house wall. But here the cylinder top is open to the atmosphere and there is no well for a condenser. The engine is not the only point of interest at Elsecar. The colliery was owned by Earl Fitzwilliam and in the nineteenth cen- tury he brought the railway into the colliery and had his own, private railway station built. Of rather more value were the stone cottages built for the miners, a great improvement on the mean terraces found in other colliery villages. Reform Row, opposite the colliery, was built in 1830.

Coal from South Yorkshire has always been more than ample for local needs, and a good deal is sent away to other regions. One mode of transport, still in use today, is the waterborne train of 'Tom Puddings'. These consist of a number of iron tubs, each 20-foot by 16 foot and capable of carrying a load of 35 tons, which can be linked together into a flexible train. Today, they are usually made up into trains of thirteen pans. The system was devised in 1862 by William Bartholomew, and, as in his day, the trains are towed down the Sheffield and South Yorkshire and the Aire and Calder Canals to the port of Goole. There, at the docks (SE 7523) the train is broken and the individual pans are raised in hydraulic hoists, turned upside down and emptied into the waiting coaster. At one time there were five of these hoists, metal built and looking like lighthouses on stilts, but now only two survive and only one of those is in regular use. Goole itself was a company town, full of housing built by the Aire and Calder Navigation Company, but this has virtually all gone and the company built church is the solitary reminder of the old owners.

Back inland, the theme is still transport, but rail not water. Middleton Colliery Railway, to the south of Leeds, is of considerable historical interest. Railways of a sort have existed here since the mid eighteenth century, when a waggonway of wooden rails was constructed to take the coal to the growing population of Leeds. The important date, however, is 1808, when John Blenkinsop became colliery agent and plans were laid for the use of a steam engine, to be built by the engineer Matthew Murray, and for a new system, using Blenkinsop's patent rack rail. In 1812, the tests were successful, and the locomotive *Salamanca* ran on Britain's first rack railway. Later developments have obscured much of the old route and the rack system was discarded, but stone sleeper blocks can still be seen, built into retaining walls, and the line of the inclined plane that was a feature of the route is clearly visible (SE 3129). An added attraction here is the fact that the railway is still at work, run by volunteers, who operate a steam service for passengers as well as carrying freight.

Leeds was once one of the busy centres of the wool trade, but much has been lost in redevelopment. There are, however, two interesting textile mills that have survived. Marshall's flax mill (SE 148664) is unique. One is accustomed to Gothic mills and Classical mills but here, for a change, is an Egyptian mill. The façade has massive palm columns, of the style found in the temple at Tanis. Seen from the

outside, it would be hard to guess at the function of the building
that lay behind that impressive frontage. The same cannot be said of
the next site. One of the most important names in the development of
the powered woollen mill in Yorkshire is that of Benjamin Gott. At the
end of the eighteenth century, he changed from his role of merchant
to manufacturer, determined to compete directly with the increasingly
mechanized West of England trade. He built a new factory, Bean Ing,
which has now gone and a smaller works Burley Mills (SE 270348) in
about 1800. It is a plain building with the spinning mill built out over
a leat from the Aire. Behind it are weaving sheds, and it is their presence
that makes the site important, for here are all the different parts of
cloth manufacture gathered together in one spot. It was buildings such
as these that marked the end of the old domestic system.

The heaviest concentration of woollen mills occurred at Leeds' next
door neighbour, Bradford, and it was near here that a local manufacturer of mohair, Sir Titus Salt, set about building his own mill town.
He was mayor of Bradford in the years 1848–9 and had ample opportunity to see the filth and squalor in which most of the mill workers
lived. Saltaire was designed to set an example, to show that a different
sort of community could be and should be built. In many ways, it
is a success. The largest building is the mill itself (SE 1438). Where
most Yorkshire mills are black, this is almost white, a huge building,
five storeys high, that straddles the Leeds and Liverpool Canal. The
decoration is Italianate, and the same theme is carried through into
most of the town's buildings. The terraced houses are far roomier than
most of their contemporaries and often quite ornate, including such
features as Venetian windows. Salt also provided hospital, school, alms
houses, library, a remarkably fine church and recreation grounds pre-
sided over by his own statue. Salt did provide a good example – the
sad thing is, no one followed it.

Follow the Leeds and Liverpool Canal up from Saltaire to the
west, and you come to Bingley and the Bingley Five Rise (SE 108400).
This is a staircase of broad locks – that is, locks which empty directly
into each other, and together they lift the canal 60-feet up to the long
summit level.

Huddersfield was, like Bradford, one of the great centres of the
woollen industry. Go down into the Colne Valley, to the Huddersfield
Canal, and you will find one of the great concentrations of nineteenth

century mills (SE 1216). These are severely practical buildings, with few concessions to aesthetics, just solid blocks with rows of windows, a tall stack for the boilers and, sometimes, a recognizable engine house. Next to the spinning-mills you find the weaving sheds, with their characteristic dog-tooth outline, formed by the many-ridged roof, which has windows set in the north-facing slope to give an even, overhead light for the looms. The steam mills were placed in the valley to take advantage of easy transport. The older sites connected with the wool industry tend to be found up in the hills. In the eighteenth century, the principal figure was not the factory owner, but the merchant, and often the merchant's house would be the centre of a small working group, in which the wives span and the husbands worked at the loom. Such an arrangement can still be seen at Almondsbury (SE 159158) where the workers' cottages, with the familiar weavers' windows bricked in but clearly discernable, stand beside the very much grander merchant's house. Many communities depended almost entirely on home spinning and weaving. The village of Golcar, above the Colne valley, was very much a cloth workers' village and everywhere you can see their cottages. One group has been preserved and restored to give the visitor an idea of the working life of the nineteenth century weaver (SE 095160). The main cottage itself is distinctly cramped with a stone-flagged room at ground floor level that served as kitchen, living room and workroom for the wife and children. Here the wool was carded – that is, the fibres were aligned by dragging them between hand-held wooden cards, studded with wire. Then it was spun. The first floor was for sleeping and the top floor was the workshop. Unlike many houses, here there was no direct access from living space to workshop. The houses are built against the side of the hill and the workshop, that runs across the top of the row of cottages, could be entered directly at the upper level. Inside, the old broad looms can still be worked. Here you can see the simple invention which had such far-reaching effects in the textile industry – Kay's flying shuttle. In the seventeenth century, broad cloth weaving needed two men, who passed the shuttle, trailing its line of warp thread, across the wide loom to each other. Kay's invention replaced the hands of the men by a pair of mechanical hands. The shuttle was put on wheels and set onto the 'race', a long board on top of the batten which was used to firm up the thread after each pass of the shuttle. At each end of the race was a box and a 'picker',

87

Above Sir Titus Salt's woollen mill at Saltaire
Right Water-powered helvex hammer at Wortley Top forge
Below Looking down into the open-topped cylinder of the atmospheric
engine at Elsecar colliery
Below right Killhope lead mine: the great overshot wheel of the ore-crushing mill

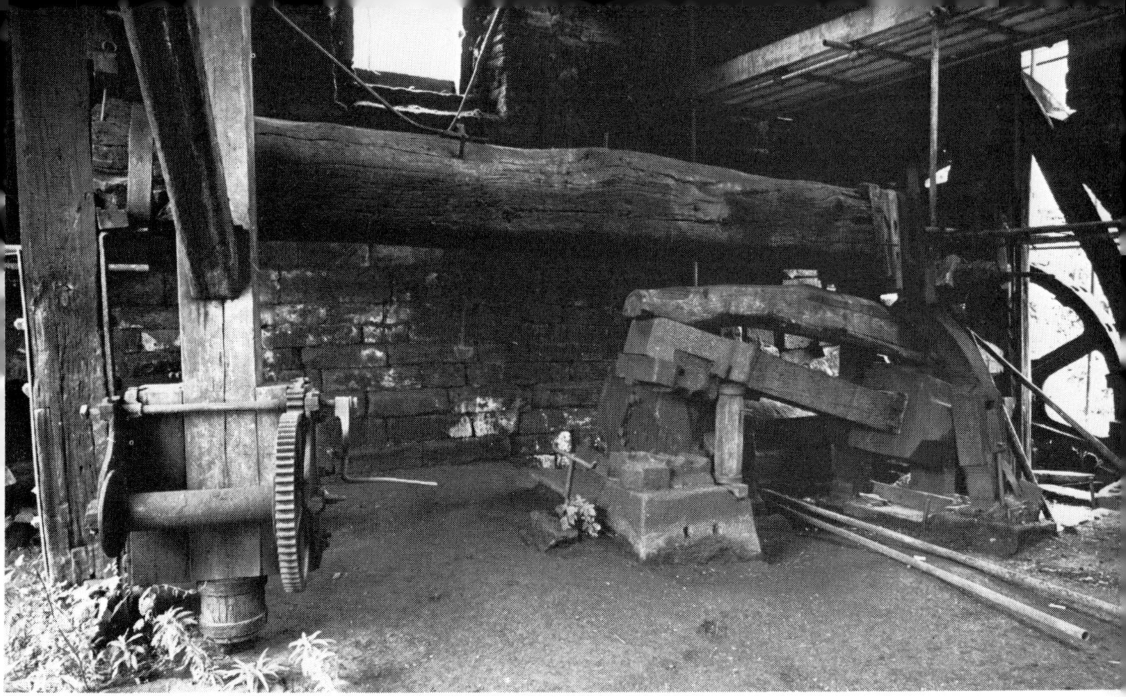

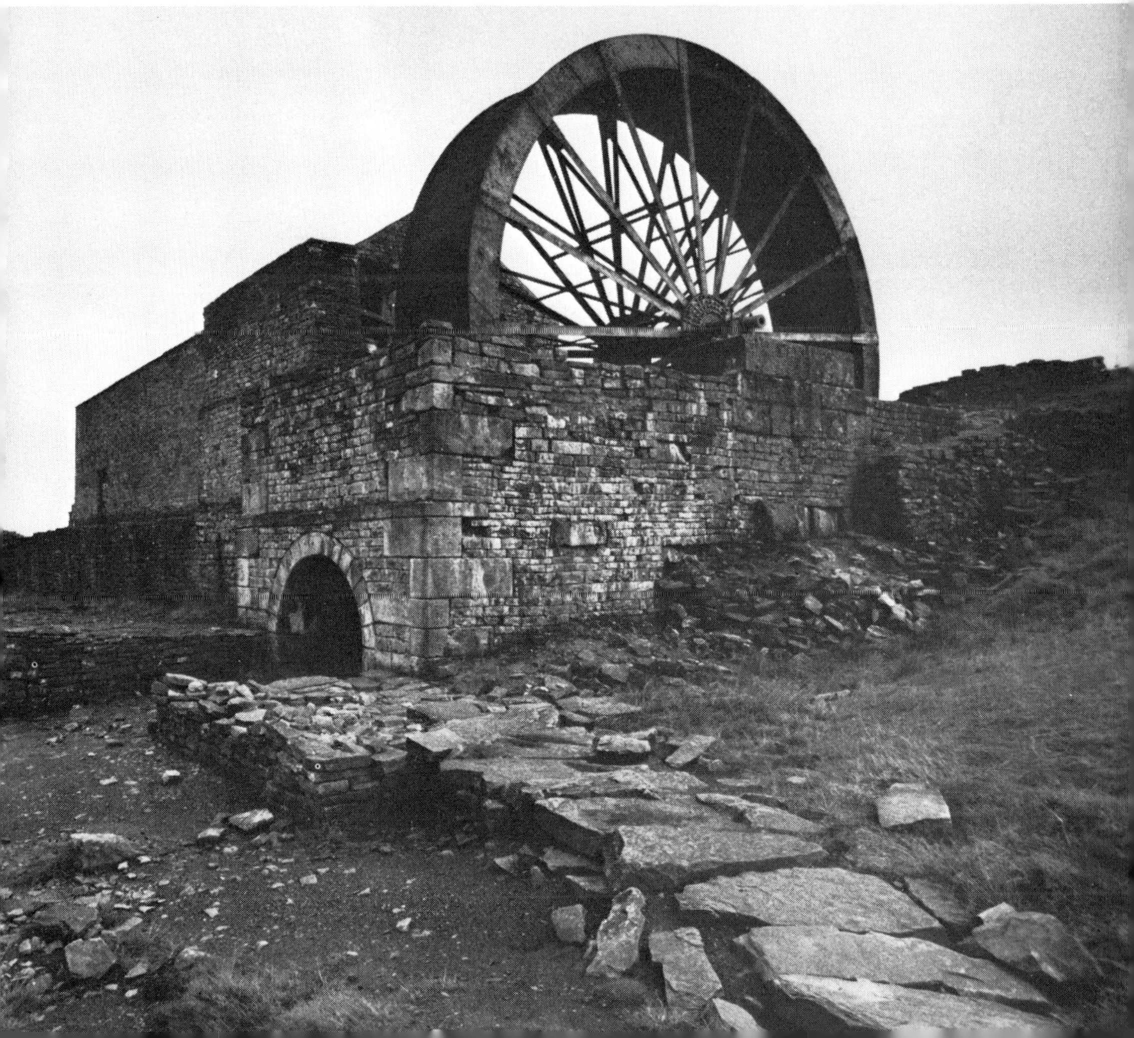

Left
Clarence cotton mill,
Bollington

Right
The living quarter of
the weaver's cottage
at Golcar

Below left
Workers' houses in the
cotton village of Styal

Below
Stockton and Darlington
railway house plaque

Below right
Abandoned coal chaldron
at Seaham harbour

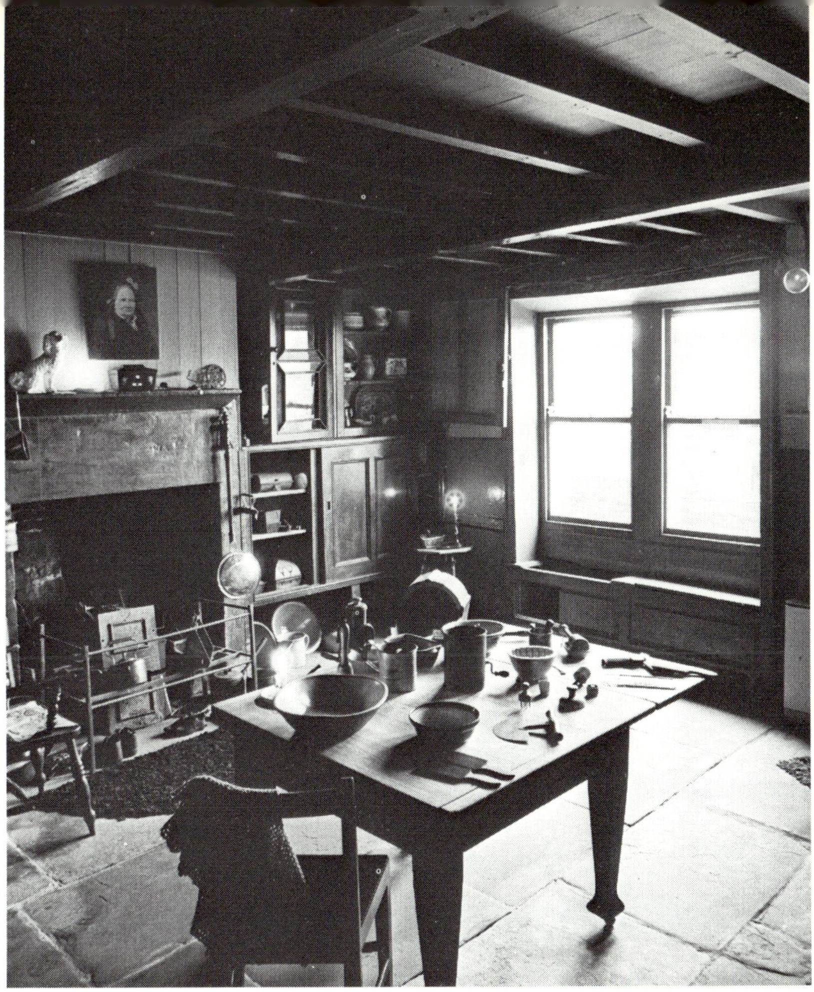

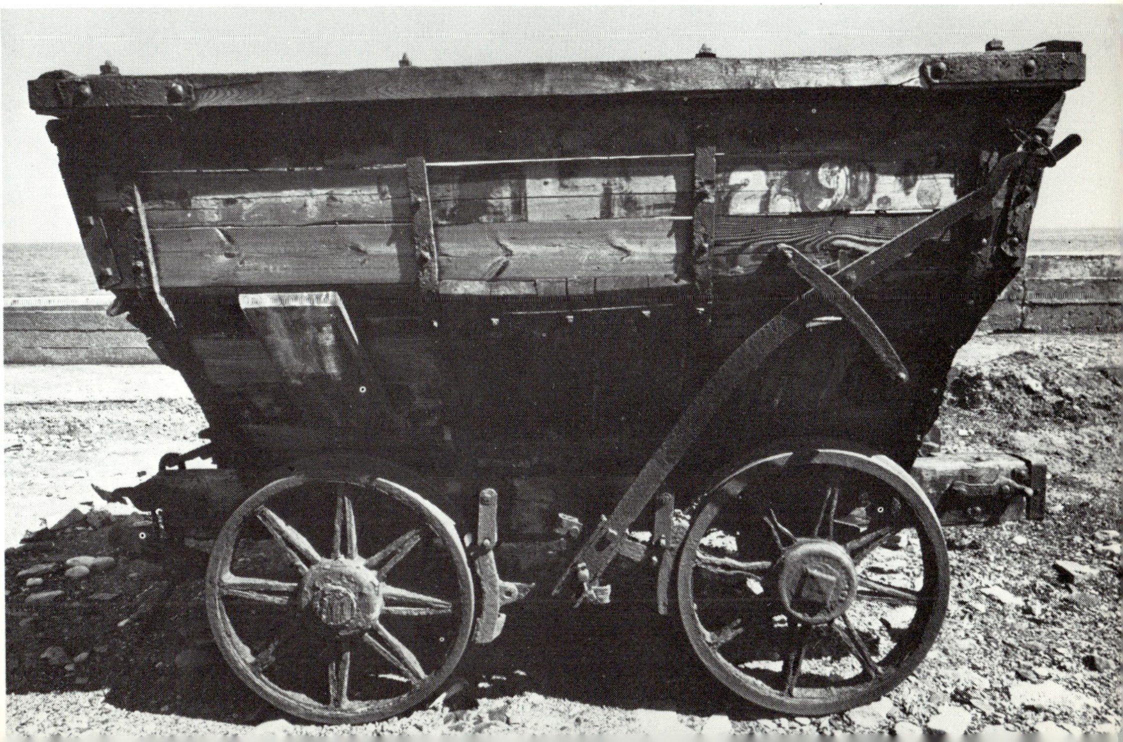

Above
Bridges over the Tyne
at Newcastle;
Stephenson's Bridge is
in the foreground, with
the swing bridge and
New Bridge beyond

Left
The hearth, Hamsterley
cementation furnace

which could be jerked by a string to send the shuttle on its way. So one man could do what two had done before, and the way was open for a doubling of cloth production.

The effect of increased production was increased trade and increased profits. The merchants of Halifax got together in 1775 to build themselves a new trading centre, the Piece Hall (SE 085250). It consists of a great open courtyard, surrounded by galleries where the merchants had their offices. Everything was done in the grand style. Entrance was through a wide doorway, topped by a cupola and a weather vane in the shape of a fleece. Around the cobbled yard, the galleries were also given an ornamental treatment, with rusticated pillars on the ground floor and Tuscan columns above.

West of Halifax, wool begins to give way to cotton, but before turning in that direction we shall turn back to look at a few sites unconnected with the wool trade. Sowerby Bridge is a place that has become more important in recent years. Once it was only one of a number of canal basins, around which warehouses were built, often with covered loading bays. The supreme example was Ellesmere Port in Cheshire, still of interest as the home of a new canal boat museum, but the magnificent warehouses were burned down. So here is one of the survivors. The basin (SE 059238) marks the meeting place of the Calder and Hebble Navigation and the Rochdale Canal. The visual attraction of these buildings comes from the contrast between the tall vertical walls and the wide arches under which boats could be floated for loading under cover. The largest of the group straddles the strip of land between the two stretches of water, repeating the arch on land as well as over the water.

From canals to railways and the mile-long Crimple viaduct (SE 3253) that was built to carry the Harrogate branch of the York and North Midland Railway across Crimple Beck and the long defunct main line from Leeds to Thirsk. In 1847, shortly after its opening, it was described as 'a stupendous work of beautiful proportion and great height'. I see no reason to quarrel with that. Not so far away, in York, is the new railway museum, housed in converted engine sheds. This location is one of the museum's great virtues, for locomotives are grouped around one of the big turn-tables, while the other rolling stock is set round the second. The exhibits can be transformed from static to mobile and locomotives can, and do, steam out of their sheds to show their paces on the permanent way. It is even hoped that one day the most famous of them all, the record-breaking *Mallard*, which in 1938 reached a speed of 127 mph, will again be seen under steam. This is not the place for a long discussion of museums, but anyone with a faint interest in railway history cannot help but enjoy the York museum.

The last site in this central part of Yorkshire takes us, conveniently, back to textiles. Foster Beck Mill at Pateley Bridge (SE 148664) was a flax mill. The first successful flax-spinning machine was introduced in 1790 by Matthew Murray – the locomotive engineer of Middleton Railway – at a time when mechanization was badly needed if the linen industry was to have any hope of competing with cotton. Nothing remains of the machinery at Foster Beck, which would be just another plain, two-storey stone mill were it not for the magnificent overshot water wheel that reaches to the full height of the building – one of the finest of its kind in Britain.

Returning to the Pennines, one returns to the area where wool and cotton meet. By the time you have travelled as far as Hebden Bridge, cotton has become the dominant industry. Here, in a very small area, the whole history of that development can be seen in microcosm. The story properly begins with the oldest settlement, the village of Hepton-stall up on the hill, once a weaving community though few traces now remain outside the street names. But once Arkwright had shown that cotton could profitably be spun in a factory, the focus shifted to the rivers and streams that could bring power to the new machines. All along the length of the Hebden Water the mills were built, stretching far out into the countryside. In many places, only the foundations can be traced, but one mill, Gibson Mill, survives to give an idea of what these early country mills were like (SD 972298). This is a three-storey stone building, standing beside its large mill pond. It was a small concern, employing no more than twenty or so, and there are cottages by the mill with weavers' windows. The main characteristic of such a site is its remoteness, a remoteness determined by the need to set the mill by fast-flowing water. The coming of steam removed that necessity, and in the nineteenth century, the steam mills filled the town centre, to take advantage of new, improved transport. The old pack-horse bridge and the old routes up and over the hill were neglected in favour of the new turnpike road, the canal and, later, the railway, that all followed parallel courses in the valley bottom. The Hebden

94

site was an awkward one and with the mills filling the centre of the town, houses had to be pushed up the hillside. The need to adapt to the steep slope resulted in a curious form of architecture. Seen from below, Hebden houses are four storeys high, set like barracks in neat rows: seen from above, they are conventional two-storey terraces. In fact, what we are seeing is terraces piled up one on top of the other, top to bottom rather than back to back.

The road west follows the Roch valley, down the Todmorden turn-pike road. Throughout the eighteenth century, most road improvement in England came through the private trusts which were empowered by Act of Parliament to build specified roads and then recover the cost by toll collection. Many modern roads follow the lines of the turnpikes, but the main survivors of the old routes are the milestones the Trusts erected and the toll houses where the travellers' money was collected. There are many of these houses, easily recognized by the way in which they jut out into the road, usually by means of a bay, and by the blank space above the collection window, where the board listing the different tolls was hung. Steanor Bottom tollhouse (SD 945198) is unusual in two ways: it has a curious hexagonal shape and the old toll board is still in place and still legible. The road continues on towards Littleborough and Lancashire.

In many ways, Littleborough is typical of the small, early Lancashire cotton town. Clough Mill (SD 932177) on the edge of the town is a crumbling, two-storey, wooden-framed building, that stands by the stream that once drove its machinery. Along the water course, the remains of sluices can be found and on the hillside, the scattered weavers' cottages can be seen. Nearby Wardle is very similar, and here development was successful enough for new weavers' cottages to be built in the town centre (SD 912167). Wardle Mill (SD 911170) is an attractive little building, with an 1815 date plaque, but something of an anachronism, for this was a woollen mill surviving in a predominantly cotton area. There are many mills here, some in use, most inactive yet, paradoxically, the one which gives the clearest idea of the power needed by the new industry is probably the most derelict. The mill at Great Harworth (SD 905160) is down to its foundations, but the vast mill pond with its massive drop is still there, and so too is the separate stack and the long flues from the later steam engine's boiler house.

The North

Cotton villages grew into cotton towns, such as Rochdale, where the early water-powered mills strung out along the Roch and the later steam mills followed the Rochdale Canal. The earliest steam engines used in mills were beam engines, adapted for rotary motion by use of a simple crank and a flywheel. Later engines made greater use of the expansive power of steam by coupling together two cylinders, one high pressure and the other low pressure and later, horizontal engines replaced the bulky beam engines. Mill engine improvement continued throughout the nineteenth century and reached its peak with engines such as the Dee Mill engines at Shaw, near Rochdale (SD 944090). This pair were built in 1907 by Scott and Hodgson, and fortunately they are to be preserved. They are twin tandem engines – that is, the two cylinders are set in line and share a common piston rod. Between the two engines is the massive 84-ton flywheel, which is grooved to take cables that carried the drive to different parts of the mill. There were variations in the cylinder arrangements in other compound mill engines: there were vertical compounds, triple expansion engines, with a third cylinder between the high and low pressure cylinders, and cross-compounds, where the two cylinders were set side by side with the flywheel in between. The boilers at Shaw were required to supply steam at a pressure of 200 psi. This was a very high pressure, and the need for this sort of pressure was the starting point for the development of the Lancashire boiler. This was built with twin fire-boxes and was so effective that Lancashire boilers found their way all over the country. With the boilers went the tall chimneys that are such a characteristic part of the Lancashire scene: tall because the boilers needed a powerful draught, and because the dense smoke needed to be spread at least a little.

The big engines were prodigious users of coal, and the presence of coal in the area was a major factor in industrial development. The Bacup area has a number of sites associated with the early days of the coal trade. Many of the collieries in the region had tramroads connecting them to the main transport system, and remains can often be seen as at Hogshead colliery (SD 887224) and Deerplay colliery (SD 871265) which, unusually for this area, is a drift mine dug horizontally into the hillside. Another drift mine at Old Meadows (SD 869238) is of special interest because of its haulage system. The small metal tubs run on a plateway and are pulled along by means of a continuous chain.

Rawtenstall is rather like Hebden Bridge, a town where the history of the cotton industry can be clearly traced through physical remains. Coming in on the main road from Bacup, you pass the long Victorian terraces until you arrive at the older part of the town (SD 813227). Here are a pair of weavers' cottages, three storeys high, built very much to the pattern already seen at Golcar. Now they are quite overshadowed by the great bulk of the nineteenth-century mills. The largest, built in 1856, is a gaunt, five-storey building of dark stone with no attempt at embellishment. At the opposite end of the row from the old cottages stand the Victorian terraces, running right up to the tall walls of the mill. The transformation from domestic worker to factory worker was complete. This is a scene that can be found repeated in many Lancashire mill towns, but what makes Rawtenstall especially interesting is its long connection with the Whitehead family. They were among the first to introduce power looms into the region, an act which brought a furious response from the handloom weavers. In an outbreak of rioting that spread through Lancashire in 1826, they smashed the new machines. But the machines returned, the factories grew and the Whiteheads prospered. Compare Whitehead's Higher Mill (SD 814231), built for power weaving in 1822, quite small with its surrounding cottages and seeming to look back to the previous century, with Lower Mill (SD 811248) built a mere decade later. Here was the pattern of the future – the squat spinning mill bulking large over the long, low weaving-sheds.

Another family well known in the textile areas were the Turners of Helmshore. They, however, were woollen manufacturers, and in Helmshore Higher Mill we can see a water-powered fulling mill with its machinery intact and in working order (SD 781210). It was here that cloth was brought from the loom to be felted, that is shrunk and matted by pounding with heavy wooden hammers known as fulling stocks. The hammers were powered in much the same way as the tilt hammers of a forge. Water from the mill pond falls on to a 17-foot diameter pitch-back wheel. Gears on the wheel's rim transmit the drive to a horizontal shaft fitted with tappets that lift the hammers and then let them fall. Here too the wool was scoured with urine, to remove the grease, washed and eventually dried by hanging it on the actual rather than the proverbial tenter hooks. Here too the Turners introduced steam looms – and suffered the same fate as the

Whiteheads. Later cotton was spun in an adjoining spinning-mill with self-acting mules. These machines, based on an invention by Samuel Crompton, use rollers as in Arkwright's water frame, but the threads pass to a spindle mounted on a carriage. This moves away from the rollers to draw the thread out, then moves back in as the thread is wound on. Helmshore is now an industrial museum, and a number of early textile machines, including a spinning jenny and a set of Arkwright's water frames have been gathered onto the site.

The big cotton towns – such as Blackburn, Oldham and Burnley – all have their own distinctive characters. In Burnley, the older mills tend to congregate along the route of the Leeds and Liverpool Canal, a tendency which seems the more marked today because of the demolition of so much of the town's centre. A walk along the towpath, westwards from the end of the big embankment, exaggeratedly known as the Burnley Mile (SD 843320) gives you a view of the best of them. These were all built as steam-powered mills, but unlike many of the later generation they were built of stone, not brick. On the towpath side, you find awnings built out from the mill to provide covered loading, giving them the appearance of watery railway stations, while opposite the walls drop sheer to the water. Engine houses and weaving-sheds can be seen in plenty. Blackburn is, in some ways, similar, in that the nineteenth-century mills follow the line of the canal. As at Burnley, there are a number of attractive, stone-built mills, mostly in the Nova Scotia area, around the canal locks (SD 678268), but elsewhere the large red brick mill predominates. By the middle of the Victorian age, there was a certain standardization about mill design that lasted into the twentieth century. The main building, the spinning mill, is a square, multi-storeyed block with a soaring chimney at its side. Sometimes there is a little embellishment, as with Imperial Mills (SD 690284), where the name is picked out in contrasting yellow brick. Beside the spinning-mill are the single-storey weaving-sheds, and around it all the houses are set out in regular rows. Seen from the top of the hills around the town, it is the regularity of street patterns, only broken by the tall shapes of mills jutting out like islands in the waves that is immediately striking. Oldham takes up and amplifies the Blackburn story, with an even greater concentration of mills.

Bleaching was an important part of the cotton manufacturing process. One of the most interesting early bleachworks to survive is the

Wallsuches works in Horwich (SD 652118). It was begun by the Ridg-
way brothers in 1777 and was among the first to make use of the discovery of chlorine in 1774 and the subsequent manufacture of bleaching
powder. The cloth was pulled through a succession of vats where it
was soaked and heated with the chemicals. Bleachworks were great
users of water, both to turn the wheels for power and as a constituent
of the chemical processing. Later, Wallsuches introduced a Boulton
and Watt engine to the works. The main block is four storey, stone
built and, though much altered, appears to be basically eighteenth-
century. The smaller block next to it, with its semicircular arched windows and bell tower is certainly early.

To the south, Newton-le-Willows is a town with a long association
with the railways. Robert Stephenson came here in 1830 with Charles
Taylor and began the Vulcan works. This was one of the earliest works
begun specifically to make locomotives, and they were soon fulfilling
orders for a variety of companies, including *Premier* and *Vulcan* for
Brunel's Great Western. The works have been rebuilt over the years,
but Vulcan village, built to house the local workers survives (SJ 5994).
Newton is also notable for its connections with the Liverpool and Manchester Railway, the first to be specially built for passenger-carrying
trains. The Sankey Brook is crossed by a tall viaduct of nine arches
(SJ 569949), a handsome structure in the Classical style with engaged
columns and a dentilled cornice. At the junction with the Warrington
and Newton Railway stands Earlestown Station (SJ 578951), which is
notable for its Tudor waiting room.

Manchester seems to have had the knack of collecting transport
firsts. Before the railways, it was the scene for the construction of Britain's first canal, the first to take a line quite independent of any natural
waterway. The Bridgewater Canal was financed by the Duke of Bridgewater to provide a cheap, efficient transport route from his coal mines
at Worsley to his customers in Manchester. The engineering was the
work of James Brindley and the Duke's agent, John Gilbert. At the
opening in 1761, the feature that created the most interest was the
aqueduct over the Irwell at Barton. The old Irwell has now gone, swal-
lowed up by the Manchester Ship Canal and the aqueduct has gone
with it. But in its place is a new wonder, the Barton swing aqueduct
(SJ 767977). The engineer responsible for both ship canal and
aqueduct was Edward Leader Williams. The canal was built on a scale

never before attempted in Britain. In 1887, a vast force of men and machines was set to work and during the construction no fewer than five railways had to be diverted. The problem with the ship canal came from the need to build bridges big enough to allow the largest ships to pass underneath or to make the bridges movable. The same problem arose with the aqueduct, and this unique movable aqueduct was the solution. The iron trough is closed off by lock gates at either end and the whole structure pivots on a central pillar, the 1,600 ton weight being spread between rollers and a hydraulic ram.

The start of the canal is at Worsley Delph, the Duke's mine (SD 748005). Here the canal disappeared underground, so that the boats could be taken to the coal for loading. The boatmen used to pull them along by means of rails set into the sides of the tunnels, and although the entrance might seem somewhat insignificant, it gave access to an underground labyrinth. A startling feature of the canal is its colour, a tomato-soup red which comes from the ore in the workings. Those who are used to the narrow canals of the Midlands are often astonished to find their precursor so wide and so deep. The commercial future of the canal system might have been rather different if this early example had been followed.

In Manchester itself, the outstanding industrial site remaining in this much changed city is Liverpool Road Station (SJ 831978), the original terminus of the Liverpool and Manchester Railway. Built in 1833, it was converted to a goods station in 1844, but much of the original survives. It is interesting to see how the new transport system borrowed its style from the old ones: Sankey viaduct is very similar in design to the Classical aqueducts of Rennie, and here the little booking-office bears a striking resemblance to one of the old tollhouses. At Liverpool, the other end of the line, the approach to the city is through Olive Mount cutting (SJ 397903). This was the feature of the railway that excited most interest among contemporaries, including such artists as T. T. Bury who has left us dramatic, if somewhat exaggerated, views of the men at work during construction. It certainly was dramatic though, cut 70 feet down into solid sandstone, though later widening has reduced the visual impact.

Liverpool's importance came, of course, from its role as the major port through which raw cotton was imported and finished goods were exported. Among the older surviving parts of the port complex, Albert

Dock (SJ 3489) stands supreme. It was begun in 1844 by Jesse Hartley. The main features are the warehouses which, as at St Katharine's in London, are carried out over the quay on a collonade of iron pillars. It is much admired, and rightly so, for its architectural qualities. Often, in industrial buildings the effect is derived from pure functionalism, but here it is the result of conscious design. Elliptical arches over loading bays are designed to have space for hoists to swing and are thus purely functional, but the repeat of the same pattern for the window arches is purely aesthetic. The sense of solidity given by the sturdy metal pillars is reinforced by the emphasis placed on rugged stone blocks at the quoins. Altogether it is a most impressive achievement.

South of Manchester, across the border in Cheshire, lies the village of Styal. Here, almost unchanged for nearly two centuries, one can see a complete cotton-working community. In 1784, Samuel Greg came here and built a cotton mill on the banks of the Bollin and near it he built a village to house the workers. The mill itself is, in every sense, the starting point for any study of Styal. A fine example of red brick Georgian, crisp and neat with few embellishments beyond the little bell tower, it has seen a few changes over the years. A small steam engine was installed in 1800, a new water wheel added in 1818 and, in 1834, looms joined the spinning machines in the mill. But for all the changes, outwardly it is much as it was. Beside the mill is Greg's own house, an elegant but unpretentious small country mansion. Up the road stands another house of a very different character. This was the apprentices' house. It can clearly be seen to be divided into two sections: one part for the children who were brought to work in the mill, the other for their overseers. It is a sobering thought that as many as a hundred children lived in what is now an ordinary family home. Across the fields is the village, and whatever the working conditions in the mill and however low the pay, the workers of Styal at least were fortunate in their homes. Neat brick houses stand beside the cobbled paths, and unlike their counterparts in the towns, the villagers of Styal looked out on green fields, not factory chimneys. Here too is the village shop run, of course, by Greg and the church, the chapel and the school. In such idyllic surroundings it is easy to forget the real misery and genuine hardship that could once be found here.

A mill owner who operated on an altogether grander scale than Greg was Samuel Oldknow. As well as controlling a considerable textile empire, he was also chief promotor of the Peak Forest Canal. The canal's southern terminal is at Whaley Bridge (SK 012816) where it meets the Cromford and High Peak Railway. The meeting point is marked by a unique covered interchange: the canal runs into one end of the shed and rails lead out of the other. This particular canal is notable for its many tramway connections, the most important of which are concerned with the quarries at Buxworth (SK 023820) which are at the end of a branch of the canal. The basin here has been recently cleared and work is still in progress in unravelling the complex story of transport in the area. The route leads through Marple, the town where Oldknow had one of his mills. The mill has gone, but at Marple Junction (SJ 962883), where the Macclesfield Canal comes in, there are remains of lime kilns which he owned and half way down the long flights of locks is the Oldknow warehouse, with its covered loading bay. The canal has been restored to navigation thanks to the efforts of enthusiastic amateur navvies and boats can again pass over its principal engineering feature, the Marple Aqueduct (SJ 955900). The masonry aqueduct carries the canal 90 feet above the River Goyt. A feature of the structure is the use of pierced spandrils, that is holes left in the arches to reduce the weight without decreasing the strength. From here the canal goes down to Ashton-under-Lyne, with its big Victorian mills, to join the Ashton Canal and the route to Manchester.

The Macclesfield Canal, back at Marple, is also of interest, particularly for its 'snake' bridges. These were designed to take the towpath from one side of the canal to the other in such a way that the boatman could lead his horse across without having to unhitch the towrope. This was achieved by having the bridge curl in on itself, the towpath coming over and back under the arch, in the sweeping, snake-like coil that gives the bridge its name. An example can be seen at Marple Junction. Further down the canal is the silk-manufacturing centre of Macclesfield, with a number of mills and domestic workshops. But the finest mill in the whole district is unquestionably Clarence Mill in Bollington (SJ 934782). Built in 1854, it is a narrow, five-storey stone building that manages to look much taller. This comes from the use of long, narrow windows and a tall staircase tower that is built over the canal wharf. The style is Romanesque and is even extended to the tall stack beside the mill, which is topped with little rounded arches.

To complete the Cheshire survey, there are two other transport sites that deserve a special mention. At Anderton, the Trent and Mersey Canal runs close by the River Weaver, but 50 feet above it. Leader Williams proposed joining the two by a vertical lift and Edwin Clark set about designing one. The Anderton lift (SJ 647753) was opened in 1875. A short aqueduct leads to an iron framework holding two caissons, metal tubs filled with water and each capable of holding a pair of narrow boats. Originally the two caissons were counterbalanced and supported by hydraulic ramps. This proved unsatisfactory and in 1908 the lift was converted to its present form, electrically powered, with each caisson separately balanced by its own set of counterweights. These hang all round the lift, and give it a curious Heath-Robinsonish appearance.

The second site is Crewe, the most famous of British railway towns. The works were founded here in 1843 by Francis Trevithick, son of the famous railway pioneer, to serve the new Grand Junction Railway. And a grand junction it turned out to be: from here, lines spread out to London, Manchester, Birmingham, Stoke and North Wales. The tiny village grew, and it is the town itself that is really its own industrial monument. It is not the loveliest town in Britain, consisting largely of monotonous brick terraces, but if you want a measure of the commercial impact of the railway system, just compare the scale of the railway town of Crewe with its earlier equivalent, the canal town of Stourport.

The birthplace of the railways, in more than one sense, is across the other side of the country, in the north east. If you travel north towards Stockton-on-Tees, it is worth pausing at Yarm, where the river valley is crossed by a railway viaduct, fifty-three arches long. It starts in the town as a brick structure, striding above the roof tops, but at the river itself, stone was used for the two arches. An inscription, carved above the central pier, is somewhat difficult to read, but a helpful council have repeated the information on a small plaque. There you will learn that the engineers were Thomas Grainger and John Bourne, the superintendent Joseph Dixon and the contractors Trowsdale, Jackson and Garbutt, and that they finished their work in 1849. It also provides the somewhat esoteric information that seven million bricks were used in the construction. The last figure was not checked by the author.

The North

Stockton-on-Tees is famous as one end of the pioneering Stockton and Darlington Railway, the first steam passenger railway, which was opened in 1825. There are disappointingly few physical remains in the town, apart from a building labelled as the first railway booking office (NZ 445182). This was not built when the railway was opened, for in the early years all the bookings were made through the local inns, so the claim to be the oldest office is suspect – the Manchester office, for example, could well predate it (see p. 94). But it is early, and has been restored together with the waiting room and has a small museum upstairs. The Darlington end of the railway at Bank Top Station (NZ 294140), which was rebuilt in 1887, contains two very important relics in the Stephenson locomotives, *Derwent* and *Locomotion*, which stand on the platform, mounted on fish-bellied rails set on stone blocks. But by far the most interesting section of the Stockton and Darlington in terms of physical remains is the junction at Shildon. Parts of the Soho works (NZ 232257) still stand. These were begun by Timothy Hackworth, one of the great pioneers of steam locomotion, whose work has been somewhat overshadowed by Stephenson. Opposite the works is Hackworth's house, and a small row of single storey, workers' cottages, which still have the original S. & D. R. nameplate on the wall. The tracks of the old line, with its inclines and crossings can be traced with ease, thanks to the efforts of the local council, who have issued their own 'trail guides' to this, the first railway town.

Early railway development centred in this area because the collieries were among the first concerns to develop the idea of using wheeled trucks on rails, and the collieries of Durham and Northumberland were among the most famous in Britain. Consay Colliery (NZ 168432) is one of the many in the region that have now stopped working, but is one of the few where substantial buildings remain, including a gantry at which trucks from a nearby adit could be discharged. Over the years, the colliery buildings have become mixed in with those of a later brick works, of which a good deal remains, including a number of kilns – two sites for the price of one. Nearby, at Esh Winning, are the rapidly decaying remains of an old style colliery village, with a large amount of space set aside for the allotments which were such a feature of this mining region.

The western part of the county is chiefly associated with the mining and smelting of lead, and in the Killhope ore-crushing mill in Weardale

(NY 827429) is the industry's most impressive monument. Approaching the site along the track from the main road, the first small building is the old maintenance smithy and next to that is the entrance to the mine itself. From here, rails once ran across the river to the loading bays. The site is dominated by the crushing mill itself with its great overshot water wheel, nearly 34 feet in diameter. The piers that supported the launder that brought the water to the top of the wheel still stand, though the launder itself has gone. The four sets of rollers that were once driven by the wheel have also gone, though the mill building and the adjoining ore-dressing workshop are in reasonably good condition. The site is popular with visitors to the area, and it is not hard to see why, for there is something undeniably romantic about the sight of the huge, iron wheel abandoned among the wild moors.

Returning to the theme of coal, the collieries of Tyne and Wear were great exporters of coal, and for centuries were the main suppliers for the London market. Coal was taken, usually by tramway, to one of the specialist ports, such as Seaham (NZ 433495). Here the coal waggons, or chaldrons, were brought to the staithes and the coal drops, counterbalanced platforms on which the loaded chaldron could be swung out over the waiting ship, unloaded and returned to the high level railway. The last of the drops has gone, awaiting eventual re-erection, but modern staithes remain where coal is still loaded. Down by the water, abandoned chaldrons can still be found.

Along the coast is Ryhope, the site of a water pumping station (NZ 404525). Where Papplewick, for example, keeps its glories for the interior, Ryhope's designers put their main effort into a grand and elaborate exterior. The engine house is an extravagant gabled building with a central turret and beside it stands the triple-gabled boiler house and the tall stack. Inside the engine house are two beam engines, built by Hawthornes of Newcastle in 1868. They are double-acting engines, each with a $27\frac{1}{2}$-inch high-pressure cylinder and a 45-inch low-pressure cylinder. The beams are a colossal 33 feet long. The original boilers were replaced by Lancashire boilers at the beginning of this century. Happily, this fine site with its superb engines is now in the custody of a preservation trust.

Sunderland can boast one of the country's best examples of a station in the Classical style. Monkswearmouth Station (NZ 395577) the terminal of the Sunderland, Newcastle and South Shields Railway was built in such a grand style because it was intended to stand as a monument to the new Member of Parliament elected for Sunderland, the railway king himself, George Hudson. It is not as big as other stations in the style, such as Huddersfield or Hull, but it is beautifully executed, and has now found a new role as a museum. The railway is carried across the Wear on a bridge that has the same qualities. It is carried on stone piers to the river's edge, which is crossed by a single, arched span of iron. The main girders are linked by vertical members, which, in turn, are joined by a delicate iron tracery, based on an oval pattern, so that the overall effect of a bridge designed on a series of curves is retained.

A more famous rail bridge is Stephenson's High Level Bridge across the Tyne at Newcastle (NZ 250637). There are two decks, carried on five massive sandstone piers, the upper deck carrying rail traffic, the lower carrying the road. The construction is of the 'bow-string' type, in which a curved metal arch is joined by vertical ties to a horizontal lower span, which carries all the horizontal, outward thrust. This bridge was opened in 1849. Next to it is a low-level swing road bridge, which was originally powered by steam-operated, hydraulic pumps. These were installed by W. G. Armstrong and Co., who set up a business in Elswick in 1847. Armstrong was a pioneer in the large-scale use of hydraulic power, and the company went on to supply the hydraulic works for Tower Bridge, London. The Newcastle bridge is no longer steam powered, but Armstrong's old hydraulic pumps are still in use, worked by new electric motors. The third in the trio of Newcastle bridges is the New Bridge of the 1920s.

One of the outstanding industrial monuments of this area is the Hamsterley cementation furnace (NZ 131565). This is an early eighteenth-century structure, where blister steel was manufactured. Iron and charcoal were placed together in sealed containers and heated for several days, at the end of which time some of the carbon had been absorbed by the iron, converting it to steel. The furnace itself is a conical structure, built of rough stone blocks, with single-storey extensions on either side. The earthenware containers were inserted through hearths on either side of the central, conical flue. The furnace stands in woods beside a rough track, and is so heavily overgrown that it is all too easy to miss it among the trees.

At Beamish, the north east has an open air museum, that is still, at the time of writing, in the process of formation. The most interesting exhibit is the vertical colliery winding engine, one of the last of a kind that was once common in the north east. Until recently, it stood near the museum (NZ 220357), but the engine, together with its original engine house, has been dismantled and re-erected at the museum. This type of engine was invented in 1800 by Phineas Crowther of Newcastle. It has the winding drum positioned directly above the cylinder, so that no horizontal beam was needed. The resulting engine house has a distinctive shape, very tall and narrow. This particular engine was built in 1855.

Quite near to Beamish is another site, connected with the collieries, and of great historic significance. The Causey Arch at Tanfield (NZ 201559). has the distinction of being the world's oldest railway bridge. The tramway that it carried was built in the 1720s to a 4-foot gauge and had wooden rails. Where the line had to cross the deep, wooded valley of Houghwell Burn, the constructors called in a local mason, Ralph Wood, who designed a bridge of 103 feet to cross the gorge in a single, graceful span. These early trains were, of course, horse drawn and large stable blocks were a feature of the collieries. At Blyth, an early nineteenth century stable block stands by the roadside (NZ 277819). A two storey stone and brick building, with attractive semi-circular arched windows on the ground floor, it is now in rather poor condition. The upper floor was a fodder loft and downstairs, the stalls, with curved wooden dividers that held fifteen horses are still in place. From here, the horses were sent out to haul the coal down to the straithes by the river, where a number of coal chutes can still be seen (NZ 311824).

Further north, industrial activity begins to slacken. At Seahouses, on the coast near Bamburgh, is a remarkably well preserved set of eighteenth-century lime kilns. They are built next to the harbour, which suggests an exporting trade. Their working days are over, but they have found a new use as stores for the local fishermen (SU 221322).

The Border Country is one of the traditional areas for woollen manufacture. The majority of the more interesting mills are to be found on the Scottish side (see p. 108), but there is one notable exception to be found on the English side. Otterburn tweed mill (NY 888928) was originally water-powered though traces of this have now largely disappeared. The mill itself, however, is still very much at work, and although the power source may have changed, much of the machinery is that of the nineteenth-century mill, driven by overhead shaft and belt. There are spinning-mules, carding engines, a gig mill in which the traditional teazles are still used to raise the nap of the cloth and fulling stocks, which are in regular use. The mill is open to visitors and provides a rare opportunity to see the older types of textile machinery in use.

Across the country in the further north-west corner is the once busy iron-ore mining district. The Millom haematite mine (SD 179787) was worked right up to 1968 and the surviving buildings are among the last in the whole country that can be seen in anything approaching a complete state. The surface remains are, in many ways, typical of those of any mining region – engine house, stack, warehouse – but what makes this site unique is its coastal situation and the lengths to which the miners were forced to go to preserve the pits from inundation. As the ore was extracted – at the peak in the 1880s it reached 350,000 tons per annum, the ground subsided and the sea began to move in. In 1888, thirty two years after operations started, the first sea wall was built. Then, at the end of the century, the mile long outer barrier was added. Today the whole central part of the site is one great salt-water lake.

Finally, for this region, we turn to one of the loveliest of industrial monuments, the Lune aqueduct which carries the Lancaster Canal across the river at Lancaster. Designed by John Rennie and completed in 1796, it is the perfect example of the Classical architectural style allied to a work of civil engineering. Six hundred feet long, sixty-two feet high, it crosses the river on five semi-circular arches. The nature of the coarse gritstone used for construction is emphasized by the rustication of the piers, but the height and the grace of form have enabled Rennie to add his decoration of Doric columns and balustrading without the least sense of incongruity. It is a perfect marriage between style and function.

6 Scotland

Our Scottish tour begins in the Border Country, that traditional centre of woollen manufacture where, in a succession of towns large and small, the mills are the most prominent features. The beginnings of the change from the purely domestic system came, as in England, after the introduction of the flying shuttle. This appeared north of the border in 1788, when it was brought to Galashiels, which was to develop as one of the major centres of cloth production in the region. The Scottish mills remained largely water powered until well into the second half of the nineteenth century, the period at which most of the surviving mills were built. The Galashiels mills are gathered together in the town centre (NT 4936), surrounded by the workers' houses, in a way which is very reminiscent of an English mill town, except that the surviving houses are built to a notably higher standard than their southern counterparts. The earliest of the mills is Gala, built in 1826, but still very much in the eighteenth-century tradition. It is a five-storey building, large but not dull, embellished with those favourite eighteenth-century devices, cupola and weather vane. By contrast, nearby Netherdale Mill, built in the 1850s is only four storeys high, but contrives an effect of some grandeur by means of a crenellated parapet and corner turrets.

One expects to find woollen mills along the Tweed, though as every Scot knows, the name of the cloth does not derive from the river but from the mistake of an English clerk, misreading the word 'tweel'. However, the name is by no means inappropriate for a large number of mills are still to be found along the river's banks. One of the most attractive is at Innerleithen (NT 834364), a four storey T-shaped stone building, with a small gatehouse by the entrance to the yard and adjoining weaving-sheds. It was originally water powered, but steam was substituted later. Its attraction stems in part from the building itself and in part from its situation, set down between river and hills. The

The furnace at Bonawe with early tenements in the background

setting was a good deal more attractive than the prevailing conditions in the early mills, as rules for the big Ballantynes mill at Peebles (NT 252408) testify. No talking was permitted; there was no lunch break – food had to be taken while you worked; and, which surely must have been a most difficult rule to keep, workers were required not to crave drink or tobacco.

Moving westwards, one comes to the Lowther Hills, and the lead-mining regions of Leadhills. When Thomas Pennant visited here in 1772, he reported that there were fifteen hundred inhabitants and that mining had already been in progress for two centuries. Not much of the eighteenth century remains to be seen in Leadhills itself, which was largely rebuilt in the following century. All over the surrounding area, however, the signs of mining are to be seen. Spoil heaps, where galena can still be picked out of the rubble, are there in plenty, and the large numbers of disused shafts make it not only an interesting, but also a potentially dangerous area to explore. Leadhills was linked to neighbouring Wanlockhead by a light railway which boasted the highest summit level in Britain, scarcely surprising since Wanlock-head is Scotland's highest village. Here many of the old cottages do still remain, mostly single-storey buildings, spread out in long ter-races. A feature of these houses was the very long garden each pos-sessed, an essential in such an isolated community that had to be, in some measure, self sufficient. The solid, prosperous-looking mine-manager's house is a marked contrast to the tiny cottages. Here surface remains of mining are more prominent than in Leadhills and include an extremely interesting feature, the water bucket pump (NS 867133). This is a beam pump, in which the timber beam pivots on a stone pillar. Anyone coming upon it by accident could be forgiven for regard-ing it with some bewilderment, for there seems to be no obvious source of power. In fact, it was worked by water. A pipe brought the water under the road and poured it into a bucket suspended from the beam. As the bucket filled, the weight of water dragged it down, until the bucket met some form of trip mechanism which emptied it again. At that point, the weight of the pump rods suspended from the other end of the beam pulled it back the other way and the cycle restarted. Beside the pump is the circular track of a horse gin, which was used for wind-ing in the same shaft.

Continuing west and south one comes to Kirkcudbright and textiles again. At one time this was an important industrial area and, in the late eighteenth and early nineteenth century, a considerable effort went into improving transport in the region. Foremost among the improvers was Thomas Telford. In 1804 he designed a bridge to cross the River Dee at Tongland (NX 6953). The river is spanned by a single arch, 110 feet wide, with three narrow arches set on either side of it. Scottish Baronial seemed an appropriate style for such a setting, so the bridge was adorned with battlements and imitation turrets. One of the centres that was developed around this time was Twynholm, some three miles away, which still has one water-powered mill, Kempleton woollen mill (NX 670546), built in 1785.

Gatehouse-of-Fleet was one of the first places at which cotton mills were established in Scotland. The Birtwhistles came here in the early 1790s and established two mills, employing three hundred workers of whom two thirds were children. As the weekly wages bill was £50 they were scarcely overpaid. The surviving buildings are to be found near the river, and the most impressive is the bobbin mill, three storeys high and twelve bays long (NX 599566). Gatehouse also enjoyed some prosperity as a port when the Water of Fleet was canalized. The area is notable for the sporadic character of its industrialization. Commentators of the time claimed that industrialists came to these comparatively remote areas to take advantage of the country's poverty and the cheapness of labour. Other considerations could, however, govern the choice of some seemingly remote site for an early textile mill. John Kenyon established a cotton mill at Rothesay in Bute (NS 0964), partly because the site met the requirement of a plentiful supply of water, partly because the labour force as well as being cheap had experience of textiles from working in linen, but mainly because Rothesay was a very long way from Cromford. Kenyon was blatantly breaking Arkwright's patent and was even compounding the deed by poaching Arkwright's workers. The works were later taken over by William Kelly and the famous civil engineer, Robert Thom, who was responsible for building a new water supply system. Eventually four mills were built, of which two survive.

Moving north into Ayrshire, one is reaching a much more heavily industrialized region, which was served by an extensive rail network centred on Glasgow. Near Mauchline is the splendid Ballochmyle Viaduct (NS 508254), built by John Miller in 1846–8. It has very little in the way of adornment, apart from applied columns on either side of the central arch, and needs none. Its visual appeal derives from the great central span, 181 feet long and 163 feet which was for many years the greatest of its kind in Europe.

Kilmarnock is the principal industrial town of Ayrshire, and contains a number of long established foundries and engineering works, though they are all either greatly altered or have been absorbed into large concerns. Within the county are a number of iron-making sites, of which the largest complex was based on Muirkirk. The works were begun in 1787, but the site (NS 697268) is now almost empty. The long furnace bank can be seen, where the furnaces were built into the hillside and the company canal can easily be followed for much of its journey through the works. Above the site, in the town, are many reminders of the industry. The nineteenth-century Workers Institute, with its prominent clock tower, still looks out over the rows of houses with names such as Ironworks Cottages. Although this is historically the more important site, nearby Glenbuck offers more interesting physical evidence. English iron makers came here in 1795 but by 1813 the whole concern was bankrupt. The furnace is still there, built of stone and set against the hillside, in the now all but deserted village – ironworks and community have both gone. Around about, however, is ample evidence of the existence of one of the commodities that brought the iron masters to this area – coal. Here can be seen the characteristic marks of collapsed bell pits (NS 6925). In this early, unsophisticated method of working, the shaft was sunk down to the coal measure and from there the miners moved outwards, leaving a bell-shaped cavity. When they could no longer excavate with safety a new pit was sunk. Hence the proliferation of remains, pock-marking the land like lunar craters.

Across the border in Lanarkshire is one of Britain's most famous industrial sites – the cotton town of New Lanark. Arkwright came to Scotland to search for a partner in order to set up a cotton mill using his new machines. He met David Dale of Glasgow and they selected a site near the Corra Linn falls on the Clyde. Here the mill was built and a new town for the workers, following the pattern set at Cromford. New Lanark, however, achieved international fame thanks to a young man who arrived from Manchester in 1798 to manage the works. Robert Owen set out to build a new sort of industrial community.

Where others increased working hours he decreased them, where others pushed young children into the mill he educated them. He was able to demonstrate that workers treated as human beings were actually more productive than workers treated as parts of the machines. Many came to see New Lanark, but few were convinced. Today, New Lanark is very much as it was in Owen's day. Down by the river the mill stands, and above it, on the slope of the hill, is the housing, tenement blocks, four storeys at the front, two at the back. Many still retain original features such as the old wall beds. And there is the New Institution, the educational centre of New Lanark on which Owen placed so very much importance.

Another company town, but this time associated with the iron industry, is Wilsontown in the northeast of Lanarkshire. As the name suggests, the ironworks were founded by the Wilson family, three brothers who came here in 1779. In its day it was a busy and productive site. The ironworks (NS 950550) spread out on either side of the river, which was crossed by a tramway. The area provided all the raw materials the Wilsons needed : both ironstone and coal were mined and limestone was quarried, all activities that have left considerable scars on the land. Much of the town that was built by the Wilsons has been demolished.

Geographically, we have now reached a spot roughly half way between the two great Scottish cities – the administrative centre of Edinburgh and the industrial centre of Glasgow – which seems an appropriate place to pause to look at one of the early major transport routes that linked the two. The Union Canal was opened in 1821, providing a more direct route than Smeaton's old Forth and Clyde Canal. Its principal features are the three fine aqueducts, stone built but with iron troughs, that cross the Avon near Linlithgow (NS 967758), the Almond near Broxburn (NT 105707) and the Leith in Edinburgh (NT 220707). The Avon is the largest of the three, rising 80 feet above the river. The Leith is in some ways the most interesting site, for it provides an opportunity for a direct comparison between two transport routes. The Caledonian Railway crosses the Leith next to the canal, and the similarities between viaduct and aqueduct are more striking than the differences. Indeed, when seen from below it is only the tell-tale guard rail on the aqueduct that distinguishes it from its neighbour.

There is no difficulty, however, in recognizing the most famous railway bridge in Britain – the Forth Bridge (NT 138784). The bridge owes its present design to another, the Tay Bridge which collapsed in 1879, a year after its opening – an event which drew from Mr William McGonegall a set of verse that was truly atrocious even by his own high standards. After the Tay disaster, the engineers of the North British Railways had to change their own plans and look for ways of producing a far stronger structure. The problems were immense, for the Forth is not only wide but some 200 feet deep. The eventual construction was based on three huge diamond truss structures, joined by girders that completed the span at a height of 150 feet above water. It is remarkable both for the width of these spans, 1,700 feet, and the pioneering use of mild steel in the construction. One fact that everyone knows about the Forth Bridge is that, since its opening in 1890, the painters have been continuously at work, ensuring that the metal is preserved from the corrosive effects of salt water.

The Forth and Clyde Canal formed an axis along which many industries flourished. In Falkirk, the Rosebank Distillery was established, shortly after the completion of the canal in 1794. It was largely rebuilt in the 1860s, and in the present complex there is one particularly fascinating building. The two storey bonded warehouse is built as a wedge, fitting into the angle between road and canal. With its tiny barred windows and massive doors it resembles a prison, though here the precautions were to keep thieves out, not in. The whole site (NS 876803) provides a good example of a late nineteenth century distillery.

On the northern edge of Falkirk stands the famous Carron ironworks (NS 880824). Founded in 1759, it was here that coke-smelting was first introduced to Scotland. That was the start of a spectacularly successful career for the works. Their first major achievement came from their use of a special boring process to make 'carronades', short large-bore cannons, that saw service at Trafalgar and Waterloo. It was here that James Watt began his work on the steam engine. In its early days it was quite a tourist attraction – Burns was one of those who turned up and penned a few lines. It is still a working site, so it is no surprise to find most of the older parts gone. There is a disused group of nineteenth-century furnaces, an early nineteenth-century casting shop and the main offices, which were built in the 1870s, and are very much in the style of that period. One piece of history can be found embedded in the wall, the plate from the cylinder of Watt's first engine. Other reminders are the carronades that stand outside one of the entrances. Today, Carron is less militant, turning out bathtubs and cookers.

Glasgow has a wealth of industrial remains, but the list needs constantly to be revised as the old disappears with modernization and redevelopment. Some of the industries most closely connected with the development of the city are precisely the ones which have least to show that can interest the historian, the shipyards of the Clyde being the most obvious example. The same is true, in large measure, of the chemical industry. The main areas that do have visible remains are engineering, transport and textiles. The first two combine at Port Dundas, the terminal of the Forth and Clyde Canal (NS 5967). The basin is surrounded by a number of fine buildings, including the Company offices, elegant enough to be taken for a prosperous town house, and the warehouses among which is that of the Carron Company, built in the early nineteenth century. Nearby (NS 592667) is the site of the Eagle Foundry, which dates back to the early years of the last century, but which was transformed into a chemical works at the end of it. It is typical of the small factories that once proliferated in this area. An engineering works that is far from small is the Singer Sewing Machine works at Clydebank. The domestic sewing machine was the invention of Isaac Singer, a shopkeeper in Boston, Massachusetts who produced his first machine in 1851. Sewing machine manufacture became a major industry in America, and by the 1870s it was also firmly established in Germany. The Glasgow works were built a little later and completed in 1884. They were a vast concern, with buildings executed in the then popular Renaissance style. In their heyday they employed six thousand workers who turned out eight thousand machines a week. One of the main features, the clock tower with its huge clock, has gone, but otherwise the external appearance of the works has changed little in nearly a century.

Textiles were for many years an important part of the Glasgow industrial scene and no textile works was ever built in quite such an exotic style as the Templeton Carpet Factory on Glasgow Green (NS 598645). Built at the end of the nineteenth century, it is a riotous mixture of Romanesque and Gothic, with a touch of Moorish thrown in for good measure. It almost defies description. It is basically built of red brick, a four-storey building with a staircase tower at the corner. Every decorative technique has been used to enliven the façade – patterned

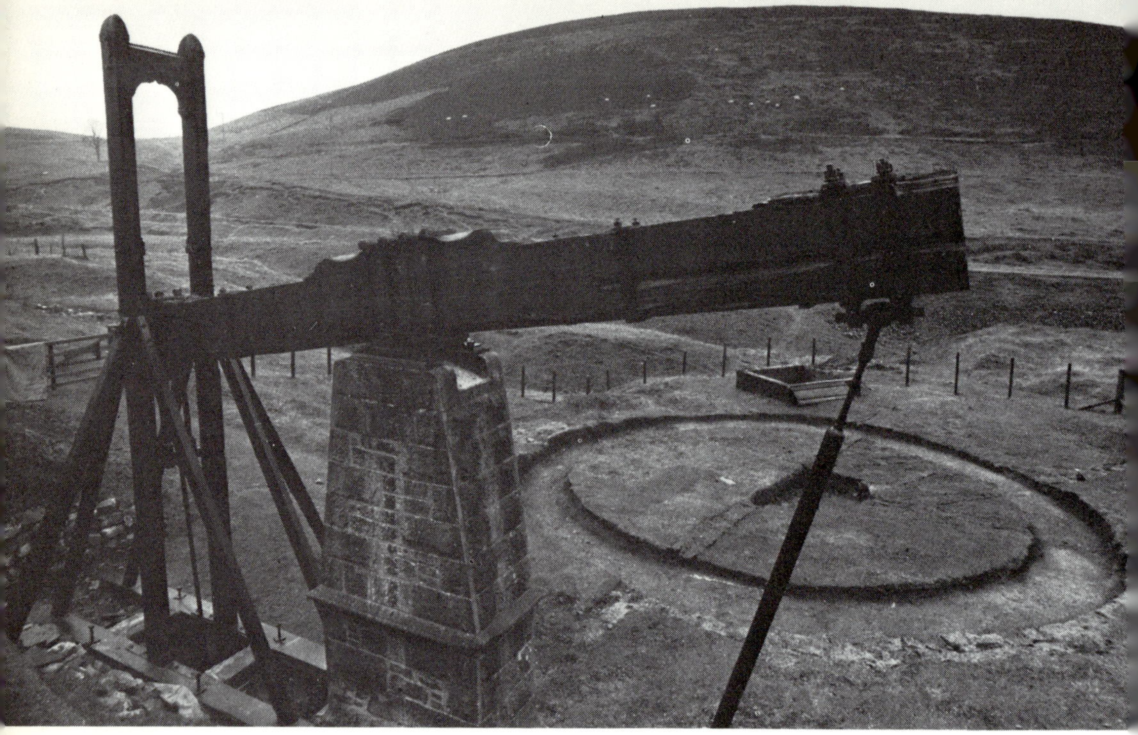

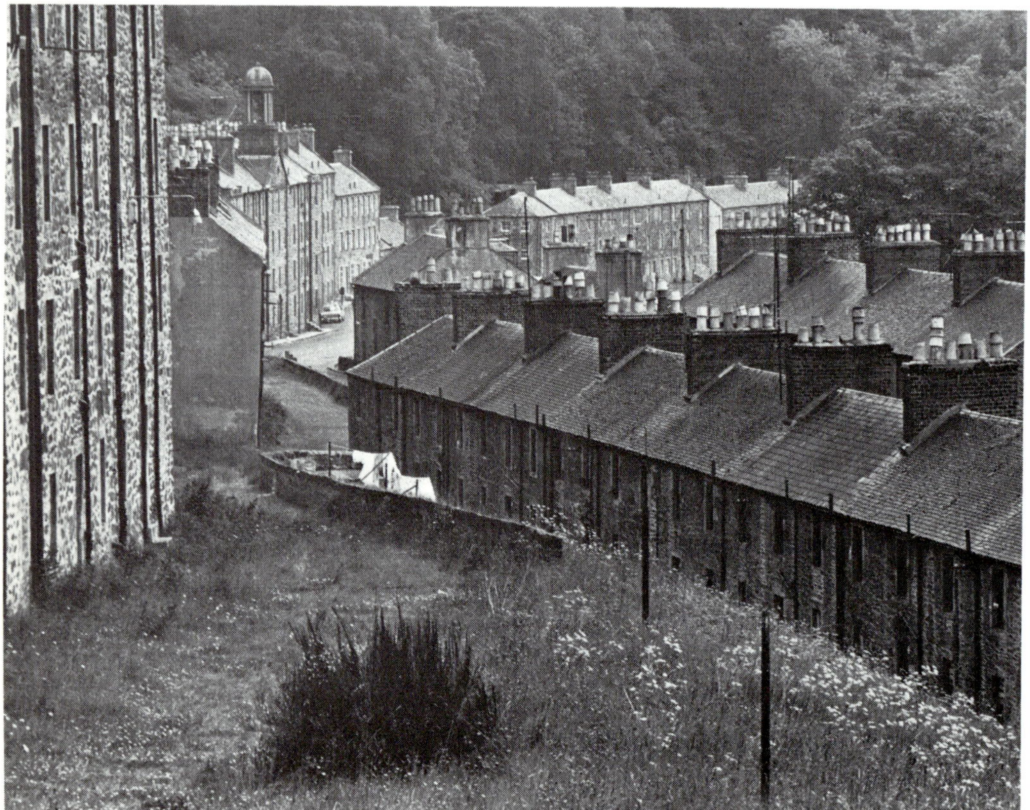

Left
The water bucket pump,
Wanlockhead, with the
track of the horse gin
and the shaft beyond it

Left
Looking across the
tenements to Owen's
Institution, New Lanark

Right
The exotic splendour of
Templeton carpet factory,
Glasgow

Top Coates' thread mill, Paisley
Bottom Bonded warehouse of the Rosebank Distillery
beside the Forth and Clyde Canal, Falkirk

brick work, tiles, mosaic, pinnacles and turrets, all reminiscent of an Eastern mosque, while the circular and arched windows are medieval European. It is either a brilliant amalgam or an incoherent disaster depending on your point of view. It is certainly unique.

After Templeton, almost anything might seem tame by comparison, but at Paisley to the west of Glasgow are cotton mills which are among the best examples of nineteenth-century mill building to be found any-where in Britain. They were built by the famous thread manufacturers, Coats, and there are three sets of mill buildings (NS 484646, 490635 and 467634). The first, Anchor Mills, were built in two red brick ranges in the 1870s. They were named Atlantic and Pacific, appropriate titles for a concern which brought in raw material from America and sent the finished product around the world. The style of the buildings, how-ever, does not reflect the names but is the simplified Romanesque that was so common at the time. There is, however, one novel construction feature: the hollow iron columns that support the wooden beams are used as roof drains. The two ranges were joined in 1882 by a central tower block, so that they now form one magnificent group that speaks volumes about the wealth and importance of the Victorian cotton trade. Mile End Mill, completed at the very end of the century, was part of the same group and shares the same qualities of solid dignity, four-square red brick with corner towers and a neat balustrade to top off the four floors. Oldest of the mills is the stone-built Fergusie factory, which goes right back to the days when Coats were still establishing their business. The first part was begun in 1826 and extensions were added right through to 1887. Yet there is an overall unity about the mill, which at its peak, at the end of the last century, employed ten thousand workers. The appearance of mills such as these was intended, as with the great Victorian town halls, as a visual proclamation of suc-cess and prosperity. But, in a sense, their very size is their undoing: details which give an air of richness to Georgian mills are lost in the functional regularity that characterizes the later mills. The difference can clearly be seen by a visit to nearby Barrhead. This is the site of one of Scotland's earliest cotton mills, which is now in a sadly ruinous condition (NS 507592), but nearby is another eighteenth century mill (NS 498588), which is quite large for the period, but in good condition, and shows how a sense of proportion can ensure that detail is not lost, however big the building.

Scotland

The big mills of Glasgow and Paisley represent the later development of the Scottish textile industry, but for centuries before that time it had been firmly based on domestic manufacture. Many of the villages in the Sterling area were handloom weaving communities. A very good example of early weavers' cottages can be found in a terrace at Torbrex (NS 7891). Dating from the mid–eighteenth century, these are very different from their English equivalents. They are single storey, solid, stone cottages, where the workshop sections can still be identified by the long lintels under the eaves. The amount of living space was very limited. The area also had a heavy concentration of another group of domestic workers, the nailers. At Chartershill (NS 792901), close by the new road development is a group of single-storey nailers' cottages, behind which are the small outhouses where the nails were hammered out on the anvils, at a rate of more than a thousand per day. Other groups can be seen at Bannockburn.

Across the Forth is the important coalfield of Clackmannan, with Alloa as the main industrial centre. The glass industry was established here by Danish workmen in the 1750s, and two very well preserved glass cones still stand (NS 880924). The older of the two, now disused, probably dates from this period. The lower part of the cone, with its arched entrances, is stone, while the rest is brick. Alloa also boasts one of the country's oldest breweries, founded by George Younger in the 1740s, though the present buildings are of much later date. Beer drinkers, as well as industrial archaeologists, might care to note that this was the home of India Pale Ale, the original IPA. On the coalfield itself, one of the more interesting survivors is the Alloa tramway, which was built in Alloa in 1768 to join the pits to the glassworks and the distillery. Much of its path can be followed, including two tunnels in the town centre, each 40 feet long (NS 8993). Originally it was laid with wooden rails, but these were changed for metal in the early nineteenth century.

To the east, the Kingdom of Fife is an area exceptionally rich in the remains of the old domestic weaving industry. There are so many cottages in so many towns and villages that it is almost impossible to list them all, and one is tempted to say look in any village and you will find your own examples. A few sites are listed here, selected to illustrate the main characteristics of the different types. In Auchtermuchty in Cupa Road, there are a number of thatched cottages, all very small indeed and having the large windows of the type seen in Torbrex. They are late eighteenth century, and must have been uncomfortably cramped, to say the least, when one remembers they were home and workshop. An alternative arrangement can be found in some villages, where single cottages, or even whole rows, have special loomshops built on. There are a number of these separate cottages at Creich, while in Falkland there are the early nineteenth-century rows, for example the stone-built houses in Sharp's Close (NO 255073).

Fife is joined to Angus by the rail bridge across the Tay (NS 395263 to 320292). This was opened in 1887, eight years after Bouch's girder bridge collapsed. The designer was W. H. Barlow, the inventor of the 'Barlow rail', used by Brunel. The Tay is shallower than the Forth, and even in the nineteenth century it was little used by shipping. So Barlow, and his son who helped with the work, were not faced with the same problems as the builders of the Forth Bridge. The resulting structure was neither as tall nor as impressive as the latter, but it remains a notable engineering feature, the last of the great bridges to be built from wrought iron before steel took over, and the longest railway bridge in Britain.

At the northern end of the bridge stands Dundee, the centre of the jute industry. Manchester was Cottonopolis, here was Jutopolis. The move from domestic to factory system was slow to arrive, but by the second half of the nineteenth century, the city was dominated by the massive mills and the jute warehouses. The jute was used for the manufacture of coarse cloth, particularly for canvas for sails and tents. Between 1830 and 1870, mechanization came in with a rush, and it is in this period that most of the surviving mills originated. They tend to be somewhat plain buildings, sombre and grey. The Eagle Mills in Victoria Street (NO 408308) is one of the smaller mills, only two storeys high, but it has been given a very decorative Classical treatment, and beside it is an unusually large expanse of weaving sheds. Baxter's mill in St Roques Lane is five storeys high and somewhat Italianate, with a tall tower topped by a cupola at one corner, and a second tower, completed by a neat balustrade, at the opposite corner. But, unquestionably the finest of them all is the Camperdown Works in Methven Street. Five hundred feet long with a 100-foot tower, even this is overshadowed by the mill chimney which reaches up to nearly 300 feet. The style is again Italianate, very popular with Dundee manufacturers. Of the jute warehouses, the best example, built at the same period as the mills, is to be found in Seagate (NO 408305).

An industry quite closely associated with jute was linen manufacture, where flax replaces the jute to produce a much finer cloth. At Glamis is one of the few surviving lint mills (NO 387466). Here the raw flax was 'scrutched', fed into rotating blades, so that it ended up as a fibrous mass that could be drawn out into skeins. The mill still has its internal water wheel, but is now used as a saw mill. The building itself is plain and functional. Nearby in Jericho (NO 408478) were weavers' cottages.

Glamis has associations with Macbeth, and it is near to that unjustly maligned monarch's castle that one finds a small town of considerable importance in the history of the Scottish textile industry. This was one of the sites where Arkwright, with Scottish partners, established a cotton mill and a new community – Stanley. The first mill was completed in 1790 (NS 881424). The structure contains many of the features common to mills of this period. It is tall and narrow, six storeys high, similar in many ways to North Mill, Belper, being built of stone up to first floor level and continued in brick above. It has the familiar segmented arched windows and two small bell cotes. Unlike the Belper mill, it is not fireproof, consisting of wooden floors supported by cast-iron beams. Two further mills were added in the middle of the nineteenth century. A remarkable feature of the site is the water supply system. Three tunnels, about 250 yards long, brought water from the Tay to turn the wheels of Stanley Mill. The town developed round the mill, and again the similarities between this and Arkwright's English mill town are striking. Where New Lanark's stone tenements are very much in a Scottish tradition, these two storey brick terraces are closer to the model of Cromford.

A second mill was built on the edge of the Highlands at Deanston (NS 715015) at much the same time. It stands on the River Teith and was built by the Buchanans in 1785. It is a six-storey building, built on an L-shaped plan from the very attractive local red sandstone. However, later alterations make this mill and its surroundings somewhat less interesting than Stanley.

The Highland regions are, as one would expect, less well endowed with industrial remains than their neighbours to the south – but not, by any means, totally bereft. Transport systems are particularly interesting. The Crinan Canal, begun in 1793, was built as a ship canal at a time when, in England, the narrow canal was still predominant. It joins the Sound of Jura to Loch Fyne, and so eliminates the long sea passage round the Mull of Kintyre. The canal was built by James Hollingsworth, under the direction of John Rennie. It has few spectacular features, although the dock and sea locks at Lochgilphead are very impressive works, when compared with anything that was being built on the rest of the canal system in the 1790s (NR 852852). Being a ship canal, it was provided with a number of movable bridges, and these are accompanied by bridge-keepers' cottages, built in the vernacular of the region, with a habitable attic storey, marked by dormer windows. The cottages are often built on to the canal bank, creating an extra basement space which can be used for stabling or storage.

Transport in the whole Highland region was greatly improved in the early eighteenth century, not from any desire to improve the commercial life of the country, but in order to ease its subjection by the English army. The results, however, were beneficial in the long term, whatever the original intent. The name most closely associated with road building in the Highlands is that of General Wade. Between 1726 and 1737, he was responsible for the construction of two hundred miles of new roads. This involved a good deal of bridge building, and the finest to survive is the bridge at Aberfeldy (NN 851493). If the design of the bridge, with its four obelisks to decorate the parapet, seems more elegant than strict military necessity would demand, then this is probably because William Adam had a hand in its design.

Wade's contribution to the improvement of Highland transport was not matched until Telford began his great period of work on roads and canals in Scotland. His work was intended to fulfil two functions: to improve transport and to provide work for a destitute region, establishing a New Deal a century before Roosevelt thought of the idea. The greatest achievement, in terms of engineering, was the Caledonian Canal. Completed in 1822, it carved a route across the centre of the country from Fort William in the west to Inverness in the east. It was an engineering triumph, but a financial disaster. The Caledonian Canal can be seen as the culmination of the great canal building period that began with the opening of the Bridgewater in 1761. Where the early canals had been built with little more than spade and barrow and the strength of a man's arms, the Caledonian employed mechanical dredgers, specially laid railways and steam-powered pumps. There are three special places of interest along the route. Near Fort William at Banavie is the great flight of eight ship locks, known as Neptune's Staircase (NN 114770), a majestic series of locks, each 150 feet long, in a dramatic setting, with Ben Nevis as a backdrop. Between Loch Oich and Loch Lochy, the canal enters the deep Laggan cutting. The breadth of the canal is such that the cutting seems far less dramatic than, for example, the cuttings on the Shropshire Union, but the effort that went into the digging was phenomenal. Possibly the most trouble-some feature for the engineers was the sea lock at Clachnaharry (NH 644468). The shore line here has a very gentle slope, so for the canal to be usable by sea-going vessels, it had to be pushed out into deep water. Clay from a nearby hill was taken on a specially constructed railway and an embankment was built out some 400 yards from the high water mark. Stones were then laid on top and, when the whole bank had settled, the lock pit was dug.

Railway engineers of a later age also had to grapple with the prob-lems of Highland geography, and the Highland Railway built by Joseph Mitchell was one of the major achievements of railway con-struction. Remarkably, it took only two years to complete the 112-mile line from Perth to Inverness and the whole was opened in 1858. The line boasts the highest summit level in Britain of any operative railway. It rises to 1,484 feet which is all the more remarkable when you consider that the two termini are at sea level. It can also boast a number of fine viaducts, of which the most impressive is the Tilt Viaduct (NN 8765), a single lattice span near Blair Athol.

Some regions of the Highlands did have one commodity in plenty – timber, and through their timber supplies they had an assured supply of charcoal. It was this that led to the establishment of a number of ironworks which continued in production as charcoal smelting works, long after most of the rest of Britain had converted to coke smelting. One such site is to be found at Furnace on the banks of Loch Fyne (NN 026001). The furnace itself is in a remarkably good state of repair, when one considers that, as a date carved on the lintel testifies, it was built in 1775. This was a complete iron working site, which besides the furnace had both casting-house and forge. The bellows for the fur-nace and the tilt hammers were both water powered. A second High-land site, however, is even better preserved. At Bonawe, beside Loch

Etive (NN010317) is the site of an ironworks that continued in production from 1762 right through to 1866. It was a very efficient unit, providing iron of high quality, which explains why a site where the raw
material had to be imported by sea from Cumberland could continue
in use for so long. Iron ore was brought to what was once a thriving
little harbour, then taken up the hill to the storehouse. From there,
the rest of the processes followed each other down the hill again. Ore
and other materials were brought to the furnace. This structure
has been restored, and the different sections are clearly distinguishable.
At the top level was the charge house where the furnace charge was
collected, before being taken across the short bridge to the top of the
furnace. Metal was tapped through two hearths, which carry the date
of the opening of the works on the lintels. The wheel pit for the water
wheel that drove the bellows can be clearly seen. Another important
feature at Bonawe is the tenement block, specially built for the workers
who had to find homes in this somewhat remote region. This was
amongst the earliest of its type in Scotland, a two-storey building, in
which access to the upper levels was by an outside staircase. Taken
together, these different elements make up the most complete charcoal-
smelting site in Britain.

Finally, moving to the far north and the Orkneys, there are still sites
where the use of water power can be seen at its simplest. Here are
the Norse or click mills, which make use of a horizontal water wheel.
The wheel is set on a vertical spindle, so that the grindstones can be
turned directly, without the use of any intermediate gearing. The best
example is at Daunby (NT 2920). A simple, single-storey, turf-roofed
building, it contains machinery that is equally simple. Meal was fed
into a hopper from which it was allowed to fall on to a grindstone driven
by a horizontal wheel. The wheel itself is slightly unusual in having
the blades arranged in two tiers. The other feature of the mill is the
separate space allowed for winnowing the grain, where a 'wild door'
allows the chaff to be blown away. This type of mill is certainly very
old, and this particular example, with its rough dry stone walling
appears to be very ancient, but in fact it dates from not later than the
early years of the nineteenth century. It is, however, a fascinating
structure unique to this part of the country and, fortunately, one that
is to be preserved.

7 Wales

Think of industry in Wales and you think inevitably of the Valleys, that area of South Wales where the earth has folded up to create a series of parallel ridges and hollows, running from north to south, and apparently consisting of equal parts of iron, coal and Rugby players. It is not the area of Wales to which the tourist board tries to direct its tourists – but some of those visitors might be surprised to find a beauty there, and even more surprised to find that even some of the beauty spots that are on the regular tourist map were, in their time, industrial regions. Tintern Abbey today is the epitome of rural peace – if one discounts the coachloads of visitors – but once it was surrounded by a thriving iron industry, with smelting furnaces and busy wireworks. The main works were lined up along the Angidy stream which runs down to the Wye from the west. Here is a series of ponds, which still keep the old names, Forge Pond and Furnace Pond, and here too are the remains of an industry that lasted from the seventeenth century through to the second half of the nineteenth. There are still some buildings associated with the wireworks, and the remains of a forge with a derelict water wheel can be seen in the village of Tintern itself (SO 530002). But the most interesting site in the area is the Coed Ithel furnace near Llandogo (SO 527027). This was a charcoal smelting furnace, built in the middle of the seventeenth century. It is much overgrown, but the general arrangement can be seen. It is built on a platform constructed behind stone retaining walls. Some of the vertical outer cladding remains, but most has gone, revealing the curved wall of the furnace rising up from the hearth. Behind the furnace was the wheel pit, though in summer this is all but invisible among the undergrowth.

One of the problems facing industrialists when they moved into the valleys was transport. They had their raw materials, coal and ore, at hand, but they had a good deal of difficulty in getting the finished

128

The crumbling furnaces and
casting house, Blaenavon

product away. The terrain was scarcely suitable for the popular English answer of canal construction, though a number were built along the lines of the valleys. These were joined by an extensive and complex system of horse tramways. At Llanfoist on the Brecon and Abergavenny Canal (SO 285130) is one of the interchange points where canal and tramway meet. By the canal bridge stands the warehouse, a two-storey stone building, set against the slope of the hill. Trucks could be brought straight up to the upper storey level, and the iron loaded directly into the top floor of the warehouse. From there it could be lowered through trapdoors to the ground floor, which is open to the wharf where the boats waited. Near the warehouse is the wharf manager's house and behind it the track of the tramway climbs up the steep slope of the hill. If you follow that track, you will find large numbers of the old stone sleeper blocks and in one place some enthusiasts have respiked a length of rail. At the very top is the building which once housed the winding gear, by means of which the trucks were winched up and down the incline. Beyond that, the tracks led away to the Garnddyrys Iron Works. Back down at canal level, the tramway crossed the water on a simple bridge, while pedestrians who did not fancy sharing the bridge with the trucks could use a short tunnel under the canal. The Brecon and Abergavenny hugs the side of the hill and it represents a considerable engineering achievement. Sadly, however, the bank burst quite recently and at the time of writing there are no immediate plans for re-opening.

Coal was one of the main attractions that brought the industrialists to this region, and one of the most interesting colliery sites is that of the Glyn Pits near Pontypool (ST 265998). Here can be found the remains of two engine houses and, inside them, their rapidly decaying steam engines. The pumping was by means of a 24-inch cylinder, double-acting beam engine. The stone engine house bears the date 1845 and there is no reason to doubt that that was indeed the date of installation. Winding was by a double-acting vertical engine with a 30-inch cylinder. It is somewhat unusual in that it drove two drums, winding in two shafts.

Iron making is the other predominant industry of South Wales and looked at purely in terms of physical remains, the most interesting site is that at Blaenavon (SO 248090). The works were founded by three English iron masters, Thomas Hill, Thomas Hopkins and Benjamin

Pratt, who leased the site from the Earl of Abergavenny in 1789. A bank of four furnaces can be seen, built into the hillside and, at the top of the bank, the charge houses once stood. The furnaces themselves were clad in strong, stone walls, but these have largely crumbled, exposing the circular brick furnaces, strengthened by iron bands. At the lower level, the molten metal ran out into the sand moulds of the casting-house floor. One of these casting houses is still more or less intact, and next to it are the remains of an engine house for the blowing-engine. The most impressive structure on the site is the water balance tower, which looms like the ramparts of a castle. This was used to move material between the upper and lower levels of the site. The weights of the counterbalances in the lift were altered by filling with water or by emptying, so that the lift itself would go either up or down. Completing the group is a square of workers' houses built, quite literally, within the shadow of the works. The cottages are small, stone built with stone-flagged floors. They are contemporary with the works, but later, in 1812 and 1832, the company built somewhat larger houses in Blaenavon itself, such as can be seen at Upper and Lower New Rank (SO 246096).

Blaenavon was linked by rail to the Brecon and Abergavenny Canal, and also to the coal mines of Brynmawr, where one can see one of the old coal levels, dug deep into the hillside (SO 201122). For the first few yards the tunnel is stone-lined, but after that it continues as a cutting hacked straight through the solid rock. One becomes accustomed to seeing the surface remains of mining and can too easily forget the effort that had to be put into the underground workings. This particular level was cut in the middle of the nineteenth century, at a time when mechanization in the coal industry was virtually non existent. The more familiar remains, associated with vertical shaft mining, can be found in the area around Tredegar. In Rhymney, the policy of clearing up the scars left by generations of mining activity has resulted in the destruction of many old buildings, but one pair of sheaves, the large wheels that can be seen turning over so many pit heads, has been preserved as a monument (SO 118064). Another monument to early mining history has been preserved at New Tredegar. Here the last of the old twin-tandem compound steam engines that once turned the winding gear at many collieries has been officially taken over by the Department of the Environment. The engine house, built in 1891, is a prominent landmark beside the main road (SO 144029).

Across in the next valley is a site which takes us a stage further, beyond the basic iron manufacture of Blaenavon. In the middle of the nineteenth century, an American iron master, William Kelly, working in Kentucky, discovered that steel could be manufactured from iron by blowing a blast of air over molten pig iron. Kelly began building his converters in 1851, but he went bankrupt and the process was first successfully introduced by Henry Bessemer, who read a paper to the British Association for the Advancement of Science in 1856, entitled *On the Manufacture of Malleable Iron and Steel without Fuel*. So the process became known not as the Kelly process but as the Bessemer process, and almost immediately the iron masters of South Wales began to put it to use. Blaenavon was associated with the new process, and it was a chemist from those works, P. C. Gilchrist who, with his cousin Sidney Thomas, was responsible for a major improvement in the process. One centre very closely concerned with the beginnings of Bessemer steel production was Ebbw Vale. The ironworks there were in the forefront of technical innovation, and in 1865 two new blowing-engines were installed to provide the blast for the furnaces. The two engine houses stand by the sidings in the still active works, which occupy a large site to the east of the town (SO 1707–1709). The smaller of the two is a building very much in the Welsh vernacular tradition, with light coloured stone quoins contrasting with the darker stone of the main structure. At first sight, it could easily be mistaken for a small chapel. The larger engine house held the big Darby engine, which had a 72-inch cylinder and could blow at the rate of 27,000 cubic feet per minute. The engine house is a plain, three-storey building, but quite dwarfs its more ornate neighbour. Though the engines are no longer in use, steel is still made at Ebbw Vale.

The most famous of the historic iron-manufacturing sites in Wales is that of Dowlais to the north of Merthyr Tydfil. The Dowlais Company was first formed in 1759, but iron making in the Merthyr area goes back even further, as the remains of a small charcoal furnace, built some time in the sixteenth century, testify (SO 035041). Dowlais was a vast concern in its day, though sadly the huge site now contains very little of historic interest beyond the brickworks (SO 072078) and a stable and warehouse block in the middle of the town. The main frontage of the latter is a two-storey block with a central, elliptically arched entrance, topped by a handsome clock tower. However, there were a number of companies allied to Dowlais, and of these there are very many more substantial remains in and around the Merthyr area. The Ynysfach works (SO 045056) were established in 1801 by the Crawshay family as an extension to their works at Dowlais. Here was a row of four furnaces, of which the arches are still standing, with the blast passage behind. They are otherwise derelict. The keystone on one of the arches carries the initials W.C. for William Crawshay II and the date 1836. The glory of this site is the magnificent stone engine house, roofless but otherwise in excellent condition. The walls are of rough stone blocks, but around the arched windows and at the quoins, the stone has been beautifully dressed. As well as being a monument to the industrial power of Merthyr Tydfil, the Ynysfach engine house is also a monument to the skill and superb craftsmanship of the local masons and builders. A related site, the Cyfartha works (SO 0306), is now part of a larger concern. Six of the old furnaces can still be seen. A good many examples of early iron-workers' housing remain. North of the Ynysfach works are terraces of small houses and cottages. They are mostly plain terraces, though often enlivened by the use of colour washes, and some have an almost rural character, with white-washed stone walls and slate roofs overhanging the little first-floor windows. The earliest, and smallest of these (SO 043060) seem originally to have been one up one down. The most interesting group is The Triangle, Pentrebach, to the south of Merthyr (SO 059042). These were built for the workers at the nearby Plymouth ironworks. The group consists, as the name suggests, of three terraces enclosing a triangular green. They are stone-built with slate roofs and brick window arches. An interesting feature is the use of catslide or lean-to outhouses, which became something of a trademark with this group of ironworks. Recent work has shown that these were an integral part of the original house and not later additions. The houses thus had more space than at first appears, though with the catslide construction, where the main roof is continued down in an uninterrupted line, the headroom was decidedly limited.

To the east of the town is the site of the Penydarren works (SO 056070). The name has been made famous not by the works themselves but by the tramway that ran from here down to Abercynon (ST 085950).

Wales

It was here, in February 1804, that Richard Trevithick ran his steam locomotive. The event is of such obvious significance that it hardly requires any gloss, but there are a few points about the successful experiment that should be mentioned. Up till then it was generally believed that iron wheels would not be able to gain sufficient purchase on iron rails for a steam powered train ever to be successful. Trevithick's locomotive pulled a 10-ton load, together with seventy passengers, at a speed of approximately five miles an hour. Trevithick was an ingenious engineer, and one of his devices – passing exhaust steam up the stack to increase draught to the boiler – could have made his fortune if he had ever patented it. A good deal of the old line can be traced, and stone sleepers can be found close to the main road at Mount Pleasant (ST 083977). Nearby, the road crosses the line on a stone bridge. A memorial to Trevithick can be seen at Penydarren (SO 051066). At Abercynon, the tramroad met the now filled-in Glamorganshire Canal.

The valley continues south to Pontypridd, where mines both active and disused dominate the industrial scene. The Tynmawr Colliery (ST 054909) housed its winding engine in a solid, stone engine house, with the date 1875 carved onto a stone plaque set under the eaves of the slate roof. The headstock beside the engine house now stands guard over an area of confusion and desolation. Pontypridd is also famous for its old bridge across the Taf (ST 074904). This high-arched bridge, which incorporated the then novel technique of pierced spandrils, was built – at the fourth attempt – by a local mason in 1756. It had the distinction of having the longest span in Britain, 140 feet, until finally overtaken by London Bridge, completed in 1831. If the high arch makes it impractical for later generations of wheeled vehicles, it also makes it a most elegant and attractive structure. Other sites of interest in Pontypridd include the Brown Lenox chain works (ST 078901), which was established in 1816 to make ships' chains, largely for the Royal Navy. A branch of the Glamorganshire Canal ran into the works under a little cast iron bridge, dated 1856. Part of the main canal has been cleared and is accompanied by cottage and stables (ST 0890).

Two miles to the south of Pontypridd at Treforest (ST 088880) is yet another outpost of the ever busy Crawshay family. William Crawshay II, who was already occupied in expanding the Ynysfach works, established a tinplate works for his son Francis. Tinplating was virtually a monopoly of South Wales until the end of the nineteenth century.

Bar metal was heated to 790°C, then passed through rollers, then doubled and redoubled until the final rolling came in the form of 'eights'. The hot sheets were annealed, pickled, oiled and dipped into the tin which gave them their thin tin coating. After that, there was one last roll to ensure that the coating was even. This particular works is one of the oldest to survive in anything like recognizable form. Here the basic metal used was iron, rather than the steel that became common later, and the power source was the water wheel not the steam engine. Water was brought from the Taf along a leat, three-quarters of a mile long, on which some of the sluice mechanisms remain. The water wheels have long since gone, but the arches that mark the tinning bays, though now bricked in, can be clearly seen in one of the remaining buildings.

Cardiff is very much the industrial as well as the administrative capital of Wales. The logical starting-point for any survey of the city must be the dock area. Many of the old docks, such as Bute West, have been filled, but the West Dock Basin (ST 192745) is to be the centre for a new industrial and maritime museum. Of the remaining docks still in water, the most interesting is Bute East, which has its entrance (ST 193745) close by the pierhead. Built in 1859, the dock is bounded along its eastern side by some of the most impressive warehouses and stores of the whole dock area. The docks were at their busiest in the late nineteenth century, when there was a thriving trade in iron, steel and coal from the valleys to the north. This increase in trade generated a host of other activities: dry docks for ship repairs were built, and in and around the area the smaller businesses were set up – sail making, the forges of the chain makers, rope walks, woodworkers and all the other trades concerned with the fitting out of ships. The buildings still crowd together in the narrow streets, but it is seldom possible any longer to be exact about the original function. One can only picture in one's imagination the sort of bustling scene that lasted until the First World War.

Like much of the rest of South Wales, Cardiff has strong connections with the tinplate industry, and though most of the historical remains have either vanished or been absorbed by more modern concerns, there is one famous tinplate works that can lay claim to a uniquely interesting relic. This particular tinplate works was founded on the site of an old forge which was water powered. Difficulties arose when the

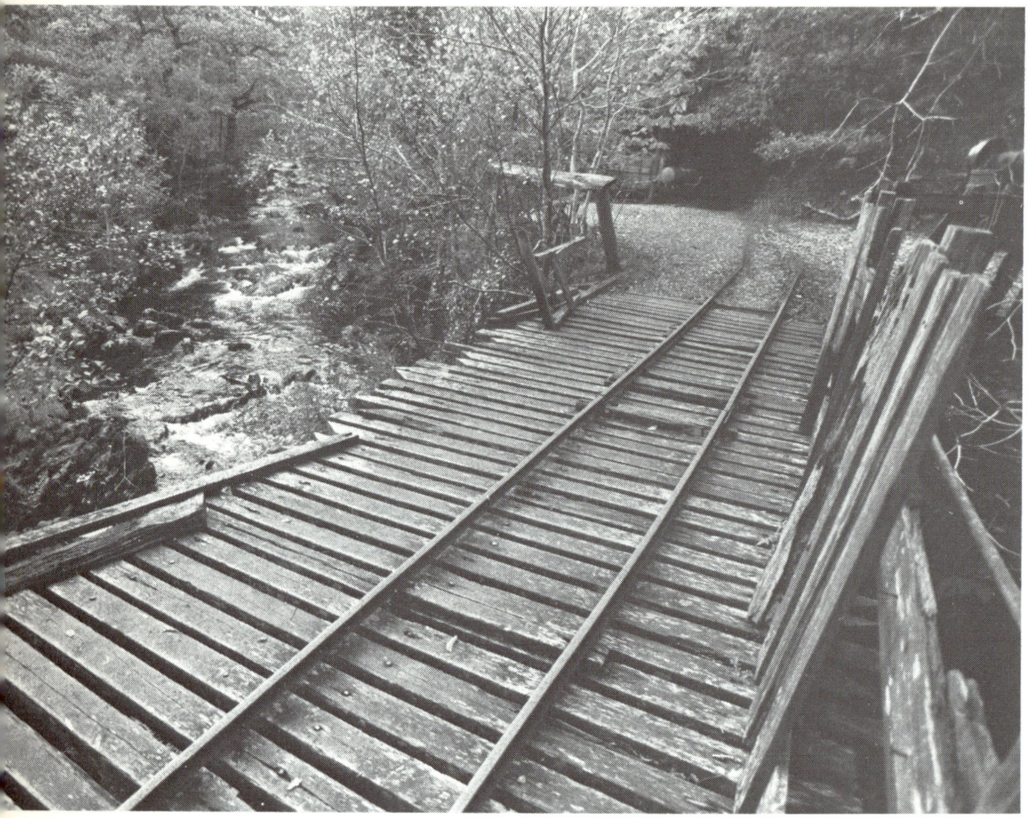

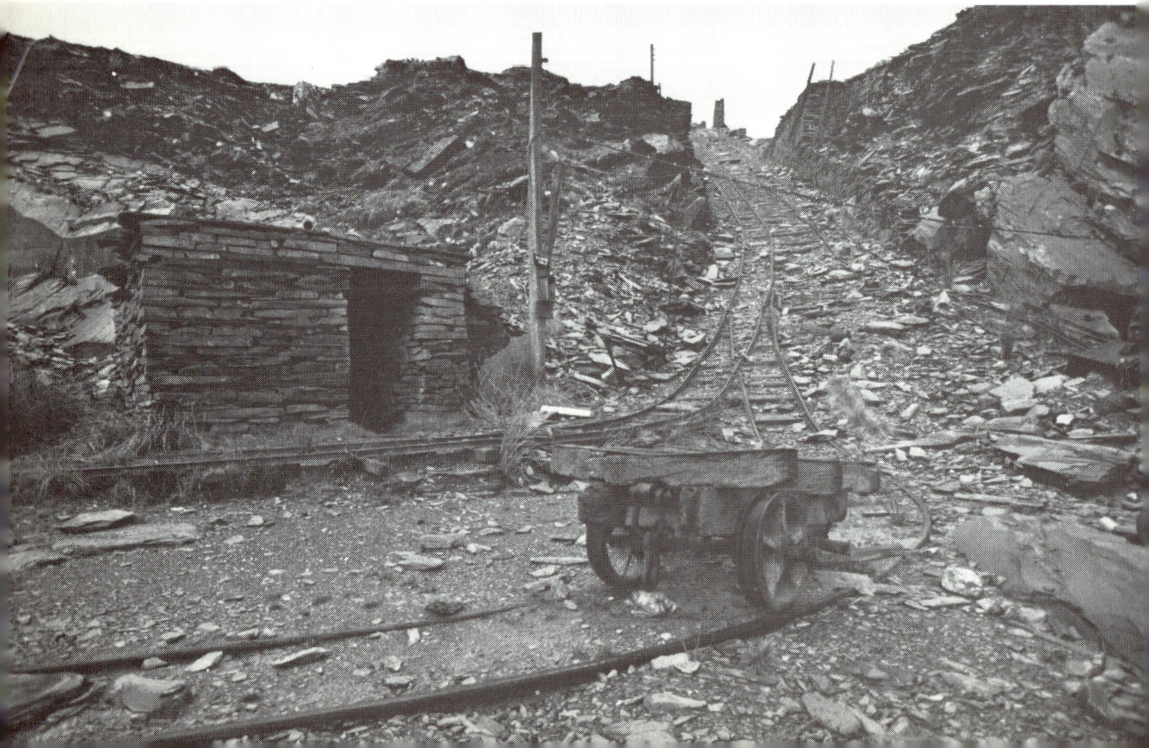

Left
St David's gold mine,
Dolgellau

Right
The ruined windmill
above the desolation
of Parys Mountain

Below left
A working slate mine:
Llechwedd at
Blaenau ffestiniog

Below
Telford Bridge across
the Menai Straits

Glamorganshire Canal was constructed close to the works at the end of the eighteenth century. There was a danger to the water supply – a real danger, as a number of court cases testify. The solution came when the canal company agreed to install a pump, at their expense, which would take waste water from the tinplate works and return it to the canal. Astonishingly, the pump has survived (ST 142802). It consists of a single beam, from either end of which pump rods are suspended that act alternately to fill the two cylinders. The pump itself was powered by an undershot water wheel. The Melingriffith pump is yet another variant in the story of water-powered pumping, comparable in importance to Claverton and Wanlockhead.

Cardiff has a number of exhibits relating to the history of technology in the National Museum, but strictly speaking these fall outside the scope of this book. The case of the St Fagan's Folk Museum (ST 119771) is rather different. This is an open-air museum which aims to recreate different aspects of the historical past of the people of Wales, including the industrial past. Here one can see a water-powered fulling mill at work, and though it is not an original building on its original site, this remains one of the few places where one can see woollen cloth manufactured in just the way that it was two centuries and more ago.

Barry Docks, westward along the coast from Cardiff, were built at the end of the nineteenth century. The export trade in coal from the valleys was booming, and the Cardiff docks could no longer cope. New docks were needed, so the first Barry Dock was built and opened in 1889. It was so successful that a second was added in 1898. Built for the coal trade from the Rhondda and Taf valleys, it was the special needs of the coal trade that determined the dock design and the principal features. In 1889, the Barry Railway was built to join Pontypridd and the colliery region to the new docks, where a suitably grand company office was built. The docks themselves cover a vast area (ST 1167 to 1468), and special coal hoists and tips were built so that waggons could be brought to the dock side and emptied straight into the waiting ships. Instead of the tall staithes of the north east of England, where trucks roll up a slope like a roller coaster, these are vertical lifts, in which the trucks are raised then tipped, so that the coal falls down chutes into the hold. Seventeen tips were once at work, but now there are only two, and these were extensively modified in the 1920s.

Before moving on westwards, there is one last site at the head of the Cynon Valley that combines the themes of transport and iron making. The Hirwaun ironworks (ST 959057) has the ruins of four blast furnaces built, as usual, against the hillside; though the site is less common in having such an extensive furnace wall and such a large blast passageway. Even so, the site would be of no greater interest than many another were it not for the very considerable remains of the tramway that is carried on a causeway across the Cynon to the limestone quarries at Penderyn. The causeway is a big embankment, stone built where it crosses the river and heavily reinforced with tie beams. Along the top of the causeway, the lines of the sleepers are abundantly clear. This represents one of the finest sites in the whole country for the detailed study of tramway construction. It is also interesting to note that the old iron-workers' houses in the High Street of Hirwaun have the same catslide construction for outhouses as that seen at Pentrebach.

Coming down towards Swansea, one is coming down to the heart of the old tinplate industry. One of the few places where the old-style works have been preserved, retaining anything like the original external appearance, is at Gurnos, just north of Ystalyfera (SN 773096). The buildings at the Gurnos works date back to the foundation in 1876 and at first represent something of an incoherent jumble. The plan is a jumble, and so too is the method of construction. The main walls are of brick, but roofs and gable ends are of sheet metal. The later was, not surprisingly, a common construction material at such works. Although, at first sight, there is little to distinguish this cluster of buildings from those of any other industrial concern, a closer look reveals some characteristic details. The engine house and the tall stack tell us at once that this was a concern that relied on steam power. The arched windows are very recognizably in the nineteenth-century tradition of building. But it is the main range, a two-storey building, that tells us we are looking at a tinplate works. Two rows of chimneys are built into the walls, six to each side of the building. These mark the positions of the tinning bays. They are built to a considerable height because of the necessity to carry away the harmful fumes from the tinning process.

Swansea, by the middle of the nineteenth century, had the greatest concentration of smelting works of anywhere in Britain. Across the Bristol Channel, in Devon and Cornwall, was copper ore, but no coal. Swansea had the coal, and it proved more economical to move the ore to the coal, rather than vice versa. Swansea decided in recent years to clear up the acre upon acre of devastation left by the smelting-works. Buildings and slag heaps have gradually disappeared, leaving only some rather unnatural looking landscape, formed by the reclaimed slag heaps. This may be bad news for industrial archaeologists, but it is an undoubted blessing to the citizens of Swansea. There are, however, some remains associated with the other great industry of the region, tinplate, and there are the docks themselves, where the ore was landed. There are the main Kings, Queens and Prince of Wales Docks, and a very extensive dry dock. There is a 50-foot-long swing bridge (ss 670928), which is hydraulically operated from the nearby engine house. Around these are grouped a number of warehouses, though few are of any particular distinction. The most handsome is Hancock's (ss 660929) built out of stone on a somewhat curious triangular plan.

The tinplate works can be found in profusion, though often adapted to other purposes. The old Duffryn works of 1874, for example (ss 675977), have now been incorporated into the British Steel Corporation complex, and the building of stone and sheet metal is now in use as a warehouse. None of the buildings, however, are comparable in either extent or importance to another set of works, further west at Kidwelly (SN 421079). Here is a group of works buildings, the oldest of which, the office, carries an 1801 date plaque. The arrangement of tinning bays, marked by the tall stacks, is similar to that at Gurnos, but here there are also two boiler house stacks, and a horizontal steam engine has been preserved.

Moving on again from Kidwelly, one begins to move out of the heavily industrialized part of South Wales, so that by the time one reaches Pembroke, with its popular seaside resorts, the whole nature of the country has changed quite dramatically. So it comes as no great surprise to find an industrial site in a thoroughly romantic setting. Carew tide mill (SM 041038) lies on the estuary above Milford Haven, within sight of the lovely ruins of Carew Castle. The building itself might not be as attractive as, for example, the tide mill at Beaulieu (see p. 37), but here the water wheels and internal machinery have been fully restored. It is especially interesting for the extent and complexity of the arrangements made for controlling the supply of water to the wheels.

Inland, in Carmarthenshire, is the only known Roman gold mine in Britain. Dolaucothi, near Pumpsaint (SN 664403) displays evidence of a mixture of workings dating back as far as the Romans and almost reaching to the present day, for working continued here until 1938. There are signs of open-cast working, levels dug into the hillside and shaft mines from the modern period. The Romans brought water to the site on three aqueducts, and part of one of their wooden water wheels has been preserved in the National Museum at Cardiff.

In more modern times, gold mining in Wales was concentrated on the region around Dolgellau. The whole area is dotted with the remains of mining, most of which date from the most active mining period between, roughly, 1880 and the start of the First World War. The two outstanding sites are those of Gwynfynydd (SH 7327 to 7328) and St David's (SH 669197). At Gwynfynydd, the most interesting remains are mainly to be found underground. The starting point here must be one of the many levels, struck into the hillside between the 800-foot and 1000-foot contours. At the 1000-foot level, one can quite easily make one's way into the hill to a vast, excavated chamber, from which a complex maze of tunnels and adits spreads out. Within this space is a system of head-frames and wooden chutes, down which the ore was dropped to waiting trucks, before being wheeled out of the mine itself and down to the crushing mills in the valley. At St David's the main points of interest are those connected with the tramway system that took the ore out of the mine to the main transport routes and the crushing mills. At the mine itself, there are a number of levels to be seen and adits which drained water out into the deep river gorge. Here, too, is the stone circle that is all that remains of a primitive crusher or arrastre. The tramway leaves the mine to follow a track along the river which it crosses on a sturdy bridge, built up of rough stone blocks (SH 669191). At the end of the bridge are the ruined walls of the crushing-mill.

To the south of Dolgellau, on the main road below Machynlleth, stands the little village of Furnace, which lives up its name. Here indeed is a furnace (SN 685952), built in 1755 by the Staffordshire iron master, Jonathan Kendall, and probably the best preserved example of a charcoal smelting furnace in Wales. It has been much altered over the years, but its original function is easily distinguished. The hearth is marked by a pointed arch, and behind the furnace is the wheel pit with a greatly disintegrated water wheel still in place. This is not the original wheel, but it does occupy the same position. The furnace itself has been truncated and roofed over, but its situation, built against a rocky bank, is typical of Welsh furnace construction. Altogether, this is a most interesting survivor, comparable in importance to its name-sake in Scotland (p. 124).

North Wales is associated primarily with slate, and although the region is by no means as heavily industrialized as South Wales, such industry as there is has had a very marked effect on the surrounding country. One of the major changes brought about by the transport revolution that began in the late eighteenth century was the spread of new building materials. Communities were no longer forced to rely on what they found in their own back yards. It is difficult to imagine now, but once an area such as the Potteries consisted almost entirely of thatched cottages. The canals brought in slate, and the change to the new roofing material was very rapid indeed. All this added up to a great boom in the Welsh slate industry, one that only began to die with the twentieth century and the introduction of synthetic materials.

There are two basic ways of winning slate – quarrying and mining – and we shall be looking at examples of each. The most important centre of the mining industry is Blaenau Ffestiniog. The town itself is a sort of monument to the slate industry, for just about everything here seems to be made of it: not just slate roofs, but slate buildings as well and surrounding it all, the vast piles of slate debris from the mines. The whole town seems a uniform grey, that can give it an air of drabness. But see it when the sun shines after rain, and it glows in the light. The Llechwedd mine (SH 6946) is still very much a working mine, but part was disused and these old workings have been opened to the public, so that visitors can take a ride on the little tramway that runs through the galleries. It is very much a tourist attraction but none the worse for that. The tunnels open out into excavated chambers, from which the slate was most carefully removed by skilled workmen. There is little chance to stop and examine, but it is good to find so much interest being taken in an industry that played such a vital role in the development of the region. The working part of the mine, though not open to visitors, is perhaps of greater interest. Here one may still see trucks on the steep inclines, even though lorries have taken over most of the work. There are slate-built dressing sheds and workshops scattered over the site.

The importance of transport links to the industry can be clearly seen in the Oakeley quarry area. Here (SH 698469), the railway main line disappears into a tunnel that bores its way under the mountainous heaps of slate spoil that top the hill. Up that hillside can be seen the system of galleries and inclines, on which the slate was won and brought down to the valley. Here are the piers of the viaduct that once carried the rails across the river and, close by the tunnel, is the quarry's own siding with loading platform, crane and simple engine shed.

The most fascinating of the quarry sites is undoubtedly Dinorwic (SH 5960). The disused section of the quarry, together with the workshop buildings, have now been taken over by the Department of the Environment. Dinorwic is the museum of the slate industry. The quarry itself is a most impressive piece of work. Rising up the very steep hillside are a whole series of galleries, linked by self-acting inclines, the drum housings for which can be seen at the very top of the hill, 2,000 feet up. On the valley floor stand the workshops, which were built in 1870. They are handsome buildings, constructed round a courtyard which is entered through a wide arched doorway, topped by a slate clock. The style of the building, with its regular façade ending in two short towers at either end seems, in its restrained elegance, to be more typical of 1770 than 1870. Inside are the various workshops: smithies, foundry, carpenter's shop and so on. The most remarkable feature, given the date of the workshops, is the power source. These machines were belt driven, the power transmitted by shafting and pulleys, from a water wheel.

Other quarries in the area have their own special features. The Penrhyn quarry at Bethesda (SH 6265) has a system of galleries which is, if anything, even more awesome than that at Dinorwic. Here the movement of the huge, quarried blocks of slate was not by inclined plane but by vertical lift. These were water-balance lifts, consisting of two compartments, which were raised and lowered in shafts cut down through the different levels. The headgear is still a prominent feature at the quarry, with a covered wheel above the shaft and a water tank raised over the top of the compartments. Quarries such as this were often subjected to flooding, and here the water was kept out of the workings by a series of drainage adits. At the Dorothea quarry (SH 4953), the problem was tackled in 1899 by digging a drainage shaft and installing a beam engine to pump water from below the level of the quarry floor. The 68-inch cylinder engine was built by Holman Brothers of Cornwall in 1904, and this engine, together with the 80-inch one built for Phoenix United mine (p. 19), were the last of the big Cornish engines. It is still preserved in its original engine house. It is hoped that it will continue to be preserved, for it is a fine engine – the last of a great line.

The final site in this brief look at the slate industry is the Cwm-ystradllyn factory (SH 550434). Slate was brought here from the Gorse-ddau quarries (SH 572452). It is a remote site, set high in the hills above Dolbenmaen. Its remoteness makes it seem all the more remarkable, for the factory is a huge building – come upon it by chance and you could be forgiven for thinking it part of some grand, monastic institution, for, with the quarry out of sight, there seems no logical reason for its existence. The factory is beautifully constructed from granite blocks, is three storeys high and nine bays long. Water for the factory, where slates were cut and dressed, was brought by aqueduct to fill the mill pond, the tall retaining wall of which still stands. From there the now empty water-course can be traced to the point where it dis-gorged into the wheel pit, which runs the whole length of the building, slicing it in two. At right angles to this is the saw pit, but no other traces of the internal works have survived. It is an empty shell, but a remarkably grand one. Outside, the line of the tramway to the quarry can be seen.

North Wales is also notable for having a particularly interesting transport history. The narrow gauge railway, that served both as a passenger carrying line and as a light industrial railway is an important part of that story. Many of these old lines have found a new prosperity as tourist attractions. The railways generally run steam locomotives, and often the rolling stock is of considerable historic interest. The Talyllyn Railway, for example, can boast in their locomotive 0-4-2 No. 1, a machine that was built as early as 1865 and is still able to cope with the steep gradients of this mountain line. One of these Welsh lines is quite different from any other in Britain. The Snowdon Railway is the country's only rack railway. Built in 1869, using the Abt rack system, it still runs a regular steam service to the mountain summit, climbing nearly 3,000 feet in the $4\frac{1}{2}$-mile run from Llanberis.

The work of road engineers is often more difficult to appreciate than that of their canal or railway counterparts, but Telford's Holyhead

Road, winding its way through the hills of Snowdonia, can easily be recognized as a major work of civil engineering, if only because one can scarcely be unaware of the difficult terrain with which he had to cope. The road reaches its culmination, if not its actual end, in the suspension bridge across the Menai Straits (SH 558712). The bridge is carried on high arches of rusticated stone on either side of the channel, which is bridged by a central, suspended span, 579 feet long and 100 feet above high water. The bridge was opened in 1826 and it seems no less impressive today than it did a century and a half ago. On the mainland side, to the west of the bridge itself, is one of the original toll gates that Telford designed for the road. The radial pattern is a remarkable foreshadowing of the Art Deco style that was to become popular a century later.

An equally remarkable bridge carries the railway across the straits. Robert Stephenson's Britannia Bridge (SH 543708) was begun in 1845 and opened in 1849. Stephenson and other railway engineers had found that the suspension bridge was not the ideal solution for heavy rail traffic, so he set about designing an alternative method of construction for wide spans. His solution was to build his girders in the form of giant, hollow tubes, inside of which the tracks would be laid. A trial on a somewhat smaller scale was made at Conway, and when that proved successful work on the Menai bridge began. It was designed with two approach spans, which led to the main central spans, each of which was 460 feet long and 70 feet above the water. It was an important bridge, so the portals were given a suitably important treatment, with 30-ton lions to stand guard over the entrance. Sadly, the bridge was damaged by fire in 1970 and the sides of the tubes were removed and are unlikely ever to be replaced.

Stephenson's trial bridge still remains intact at Conway, and again Stephenson had Telford for a neighbour (SH 783774). It has to be admitted that the railway bridge is somewhat overshadowed. As soon as work was completed at Menai, Telford began work here on another suspension bridge. Here the original wrought iron chains have been retained, which is not the case at Menai. Built literally within the shadow of the mighty Conway castle, the supporting towers for the bridge were given the full castellation treatment, and a suitably battlemented tollhouse was also built. Stephenson followed suit, and his castellated bridge is, if anything, even more ornate than Telford's. The latter bridge has a 327-foot span, but is now only used by pedestrians, the main traffic being carried on a new road bridge – with no castellations.

Telford's two suspension bridges are magnificent structures, but neither can quite compare with what must be his most famous work, the aqueduct of Pontcysyllte which carries the Ellesmere Canal across the River Dee (SJ 270410). Quite how much of the credit for this work should go to Telford has become a matter of some debate, so at the moment it is perhaps safest to describe it as the Telford-Jessop aqueduct, though there are those who would quibble about the order. The known facts are that Telford was Jessop's assistant on the Ellesmere Canal, but was called away to take over as chief engineer on the Shrewsbury Canal (see p. 61). On his return he was full of the idea of using an iron trough rather than the traditional stone for the Dee aqueduct. The plans for the masonry aqueduct were scrapped and new plans were devised for an iron trough carried on stone pillars. Argument now begins over deciding who was chiefly responsible for the actual design. Whoever it was, the result was a structure that is far and away the most impressive to be found on the whole of the British waterway system. A high embankment, that is itself a major piece of engineering, brings the canal to the southern end of the aqueduct. The trough is carried on nineteen arches, which rise to a maximum height of 120 feet above the water. The piers are solid up to a height of 70 feet, then left hollow, with cross-braced walls. The trough is 1,007 feet long, made of iron sections cast at the nearby Plas Kynaston ironworks. The towpath is cantilevered over the water. It is at once simple and majestic.

Finally, we can turn away from transport and return to the industry with which this guide began – copper mining. Parys Mountain (SH 4490) in Anglesey was discovered, in the late eighteenth century, to be rich in copper ore. The scale of mining that developed here was not matched anywhere else at that time. There were over fifteen hundred men at work. Tunnelling soon gave way to open-cast mining on a huge scale, with production measured in thousands of tons per year. At last, the mountain was stripped of its wealth and abandoned. Today it seems as alien as a lunar landscape: all is barren, nothing grows. Whole sections of the mountain have simply been eaten away, leaving great yawning cavities overhung by rocks. Spoil heaps litter the summit, shafts pockmark the slopes. At the summit stands the tower of the five-sailed windmill that once powered wooden drainage-pumps. Lower down is a Cornish engine house and stack. At the bottom of the hill, are the precipitation pits terraced into the slope, in which copper was precipitated from solution with iron, and the rich slurry was gradually concentrated by washing down through the various pits. In the village of Amlwch are the remains of the harbour from which the ore was shipped.

Many of the sites we have looked at in this guide have been monuments to man's skill and ingenuity. Parys Mountain is a monument to another side of his nature, to his rapacity and thoughtless greed. What was once a mountain, is now little more than a heap of rubble, a sterile land. One of the great fascinations of industrial archaeology comes from observing the contrast between the ability of man to bridge the gap between Anglesey and the mainland with two handsome, well designed and well built structures and his ability to destroy as completely as he has done at Parys Mountain.

Appendix: Transport Systems

In a guide book of this sort, one inevitably concentrates on specific sites, and in terms of transport routes this tends to mean selecting bridges, viaducts, tunnels, stations and so on while being forced to ignore the nature of the route as a whole. The Holyhead Road is not just a bridge to Anglesey, the Ellesmere Canal is something more than one big aqueduct and the Highland Railway cannot be adequately described in terms of a single viaduct. There is nothing like enough space left to do justice to this topic, but I should like to indicate ways in which the reader might care to follow the topic through for himself.

Roads present the greatest difficulty to the industrial archaeologist. A road that was first laid down in, say, the eighteenth century, has very probably been so altered with resurfacing and straightening as to be old in the 'grandfather's hammer' sense – this hammer is two hundred years old; it has had three new heads and two new handles. The most interesting routes are often the oldest, the ancient trackways, the Roman roads, drove roads and pack horse routes. The latter are often of particular interest, for the old routes are often those which connect the older industrial centres: realignments reflect a movement to new centres and, quite often, a change in the type of transport. In the Hebden Bridge area, for example (p. 88), one can see quite clearly how the pack horse routes went for the high, dry ground of the summits, while all the newer transport routes were forced to crowd into the flat valley bottom. Following a pack horse route can often lead one to fresh discoveries. Taking a high line along the northern edge of the Colne Valley to the west of Huddersfield, such a route led me to a most interesting, but abandoned and decaying, group of weavers' cottages (SE 064148). Other routes have been superseded, relegated to a position of little importance. This is the case of the B4027, on which the Oxfordshire village where I live is situated. Now a minor road, it was once part of the main London to Worcester highway, and you can see something of its former importance in the wide grass verges. The present metalled road is little more than half the width of the old coach route. And such roads can turn up interesting relics. Near the village of Stanton St John is a seventeenth-century boundary stone, marking the point where responsibility for the highway passed from one authority to the next. Such boundary stones are rare, but milestones, many

149

of which were erected by eighteenth-century turnpike trusts are common. They can be interesting and decorative in themselves, and can also provide clues to some connections that might not otherwise be obvious. For example, you can find milestones in the Stoke area which are made of cast iron and use precisely the same castings as those found on the Trent and Mersey Canal.

To some extent, we have already looked at some of the differences to be found, in terms of engineering techniques, between different canals. It remains true, however, that these can only be fully appreciated by someone travelling if not the whole length then at least for a considerable distance along the canal. An important point about the canal system is that, unlike either roads or railways, it was built specifically for goods rather than passengers. There are therefore a good many canals which provide a pleasant way of introducing yourself to an industrial region. The Leeds and Liverpool, for example, begins with the port at Liverpool, passes through the cotton and mining area of Lancashire and then, after a glorious passage through the Pennine hills, ends among the woollen mills of Yorkshire. There is no better introduction to Birmingham and the Black Country than an exploration of the complex network of the BCN (Birmingham Canal Navigations). Other routes offer views of different industries. The great advantage of this method is that whether you travel on the towpath by foot or go by boat, you are always going to be travelling at a speed which gives you time to look around.

Travelling by rail tends to be somewhat faster than travelling by canal, and we have probably all suffered the frustration of catching a glimpse of some interesting spot, only to be whisked away by the train. And no amount of subsequent rummaging through maps and memories ever seems to help in finding it again. In the post-war years, the main change on the railways has been – apart from the closures – the change from steam to diesel and electric locomotives. And as steam has disappeared from the main lines, so it has reappeared on privately owned branch lines. You can find them all over the country – the famous narrow gauge lines of Wales, such as Bala and Talyllyn and equally famous lines in the rest of the country – Bluebell, Dart Valley, Severn Valley, Worth Valley and so on. Some run extensive passenger services, some such as the Quainton Railway Society have little track, but a good deal of interesting rolling-stock. Details of all these societies can be obtained from the Association of Railway Preservation Societies. To some extent it might seem a somewhat artificial exercise to travel behind steam locomotives over short routes, simply for the pleasure of the trip, part of the fashionable nostalgia boom. But the understanding of history is to a great extent an act of imagination as much as an act of cold logic. To see a locomotive at work is a different experience from seeing it as a static

Above
The 2–6–0 Ivatt
heading a passenger
train on the Severn
Valley Railway

Right
Toll House at Oxford

museum exhibit. But if the steam lines are mostly about rolling stock, the remaining main and branch lines are concerned with the civil engineering of the railways. In this guide I have put very little emphasis on the many miles of high banks and deep cuts that mark the railway system. This was mainly because the techniques of cutting and banking originated in an earlier age on the canals, but no railway traveller can fail to be impressed by features such as the Tring cutting. Nor can they fail to appreciate the surveying skill that went into some of the Scottish railways. If you travel, for example, the old West Highland Railway on its route to the old Skye ferry terminal at Mallaig, you will be rewarded by the sight of some fine railway engineering, not to mention some of the finest scenery these isles can offer. That brings us neatly back to the point made in the Introduction – industrial archaeology is a subject that can be enjoyed in more ways than one.

Further Reading

The following are recommended as general introductions to industrial archaeology.

R. A. Buchanan, *Industrial Archaeology in Britain*, 1972

R. A. Buchanan, (ed.) *The Theory and Practice of Industrial Archaeology*, 1968

Anthony Burton, *Remains of a Revolution*, 1975

Neil Cossons, *The B.P. Book of Industrial Archaeology*, 1975

T. K. Derry and T. I. Williams, *A Short History of Technology*, 1960

Kenneth Hudson, *Industrial Archaeology*, 1963

J. P. M. Pannell, *The Techniques of Industrial Archaeology*, 1966

Arthur Raistrick, *Industrial Archaeology*, 1972

J. M. Richards, *The Functional Tradition*, 1958

A series of books, edited by R. R. Green, *The Industrial Archaeology of Great Britain*, offers surveys of different regions. A number of local societies also publish their own regional guides and gazetteers.

Index

Index

Index

Index